T0366541

INDONESIA

Number 115 April 2023

Published by Southeast Asia Program Publications • Cornell University Press

Submissions: Submit manuscript as double-spaced document in MS word or similar. Please format citation and footnotes according to the style guidelines in *The Chicago Manual of Style*, 17th edition.

Address: Please address all correspondence and manuscripts to the managing editor at sg265@cornell.edu. We prefer electronic submissions.

Reprints: Contributors will receive one complimentary copy of the issue in which their articles appear.

Abstracts: Abstracts of articles published in *Indonesia* appear in *Excerpta Indonesica*, which is published semiannually by the Royal Institute of Linguistics and Anthropology, Leiden. Articles appearing in this journal are also abstracted and indexed in *Historical Abstracts* and *America: History and Life*.

Subscription information: Contact subscriptions@dukeupress.edu for more information. Digital subscriptions for individuals and institutions are handled by Project Muse (muse@jhu.press.edu).

INDONESIA online: All *Indonesia* articles published at least five years prior to the date of the current issue are accessible to our readers on the internet free of charge. For more information concerning annual print and online subscriptions, pay-per-view access to recent articles, and access to our archives, please see: seap.einaudi.cornell.edu/indonesia_journal or http://ecommons.cornell.edu

Managing Editor   Sarah E. M. Grossman

Cover credit: Elaine Brière photographer/filmmaker.

ISBN 978-1-50177-313-6
ISSN 0019-7289
©2023 Cornell University

INDONESIA

Timor-Leste: A Belated, Long, and Troubled Decolonization

Rui Graça Feijó

1.

On 20 May 2002, the Democratic Republic of Timor-Leste proclaimed the restoration of its independence. Unlike the brief episode of 1975, this time the birth of a novel nation-state was acknowledged by the international community. In Tasi-Tolu, in the outskirts of the capital city of Dili, UN Secretary General Kofi Annan, Portuguese President Jorge Sampaio, Indonesian President Megawati Sukarnoputri, former US President Bill Clinton, Australian Prime Minister John Howard, and a special envoy of Pope John Paul II witnessed the moment before a huge crowd. Soon the new nation would be welcomed as the UN's 191st member state. A belated, long, and troubled decolonization process had come to its happy end.

Until 1975, Timor had been a Portuguese colony. Situated in the Lesser Sundas area of maritime Southeast Asia, Timor was the colony that stood farther away from Portugal, and scant attention was paid to its inhabitants. Foreign domination had been challenged along the centuries (Durand 2011; Kammen 2016). Significant struggles were waged against the Portuguese when the new winds of colonialism post-Berlin Conference were brought to the territory (Pélissier 1996). The Japanese occupation (1942–45) was also accompanied by severe anti-foreigner activity (Cardoso 2007). However, at the end of World War II, Salazar—the authoritarian ruler of Portugal's "Estado Novo"

Rui Graça Feijó is Research Fellow at the Centre for Social Studies (CES), University of Coimbra (with a contract under the aegis of the transitional provisions of law 57/2017) and Assistant Researcher at the Institute for Contemporary History (IHC), NOVA University of Lisboa. Research embodied in this text was funded by the Portuguese agency for science and technology through Grant FCT/PTDC/HAR-HIS/30670/2017 sustaining the research project "The Self-Determination of Timor-Leste: A Study in Transnational History."

(1933–74)—secured the return of the territory to the "empire," thwarting the possibility of following the example of its giant neighbor, Indonesia (which proclaimed independence on August 17, 1945). Despite announcing the return as "wealthy friends," Portugal was unable to foster the kind of development in Timor that would be achieved in other colonies (namely Angola and Mozambique), and the territory remained mostly dormant. A brief and localized uprising in 1959 signaled that the colonial issue was not laid to rest (Alexandre 2017)—but it left no major consequences in the local proto-nationalism.

The Portuguese empire, renamed "overseas provinces," came under fire in the early 1960s, a time when most European nations had granted independence to their colonies. Three theaters of war were initiated in 1961–64 (Angola, Guinea-Bissau, and Mozambique). Portugal responded by mobilizing its youth to serve in the army—the second most significant enrollment rate after Israel, above the US war effort in Vietnam (Cardina 2020). The capacity to sustain a prolonged war was overstated by the regime, and on April 25, 1974 a coup led by mid-ranking officers weary of a struggle without an end in sight brought down the "Estado Novo" (1933–74), soon followed by a true revolution—the Carnation Revolution. The new leaders promised three Ds—development, democratization, and decolonization. In fact, putting an end to the colonial wars was the first priority of the new authorities.

In 1974–75, the Portuguese empire came to its end. The priority was assigned to reach a cease-fire, that's to say, to negotiate with the liberation movements where wars raged. Those nationalist movements were organized under a common umbrella—the Conference of the Nationalist Organizations of the Portuguese Colonies—and imposed negotiations even where no military action had been taken (Cabo Verde and São Tomé e Príncipe). Timor-Leste was absent from CNOPC. In fact, when the Carnation Revolution happened, there was no organized nationalist movement in Timor-Leste. Timor was not in the first line of the new authorities' concerns.

In May 1974, the formation of nationalist organizations was allowed, and in Timor-Leste three of those emerged in quick succession: one stood for the continuation of close relations with Portugal, albeit under a new mantle; another one supported the integration of the colony into Indonesia; and a third one defended independence for the territory. It took more than one year before Portugal devised—in close articulation with the nationalist movements (Feijó 2022)—a roadmap to self-determination (Constitutional Law 7/75 published in July). This was only possible once all the African colonies (except Angola) had been granted independence. Indonesia was informed of the Portuguese projects and lengthy talks took place (Pereira and Feijó 2023). The roadmap included the election on the third Sunday in October 1976 of a constitutional assembly tasked with defining the future of the territory, by universal, free, direct, and secret ballot "with the full acceptance of the principles enshrined in the Universal Declaration of Human Rights." A High Commissioner would be appointed by Lisboa together with two other representatives of the local government and three Timorese, representing each one a different political party. Two years after the election, the Portuguese sovereignty would cease unless a negotiated settlement decided otherwise. The conditions seemed to be ripe for an "exemplary decolonization."

However, a brief but bloody civil war broke out in Dili (August/September 1975), and the process collapsed. FRETILIN (the independentist movement) took control over the territory and drove the other parties (UDT and APODETI plus some minor ones) across the border. Portuguese forces withdrew to a tiny island off the Dili coast, and the leaders in Lisboa made strenuous efforts to bring back all parties to the negotiating table (Pereira and Feijó 2022). This proved to be an impossible task. Frustrated with the delays in the negotiations and fearing an escalation of the skirmishes with Indonesia forces near the border, FRETILIN took a bold decision: to proclaim unilaterally the independence of Timor-Leste under its administration (November 28, 1975). The pro-Indonesian parties issued the so-called "Balibó declaration"—actually drafted in Bali by intelligence officers—asking for a military intervention. Portugal refused to accept the fait accompli—and few countries ever recognized the self-proclaimed new state. Indonesia, however, had another solution in mind: on December 7 its military forces invaded "Portuguese Timor." They boasted that they would have breakfast in Batugadé (the border with Indonesia), have lunch in the capital city of Dili, and dinner in Lospalos, the easternmost district. They would be proven entirely wrong. A new chapter in the self-determination process was about to begin, and it would last twenty-four long years.

Portugal reacted to the invasion of its colony by raising the issue at the UN (both UN Security Council and General Assembly) (Santos and Pereira 2022). More than securing condemnation through UN resolutions, Portugal managed to keep Timor as a "non-autonomous territory under Portuguese administration," a classification that offered a sound basis for further diplomatic action. Indonesia installed a "provisional government" based on members of the Timorese parties that had supported the invasion and sought to legitimize the annexation by replicating what it had done back in 1969 in relation to Western Papua/Irian Jaya: a meeting was convened of "traditional leaders" (under duress) who unanimously declared their support for the annexation. Following this declaration, the Indonesian parliament declared Timor-Timur (Tim-Tim) as its "27th province." Unlike what had happened in the case of Irian Jaya, this time the international community was not convinced of the wisdom of the move, and Indonesia was isolated in its claims. Only Australia would recognize, years later, the de jure annexation of Portuguese Timor—most other countries being content with accepting the de facto situation. This fact permitted the issue to remain alive in international fora.

Indonesian policies toward Tim-Tim can be understood as a form of "repressive developmentalism" (Jerónimo 2018) that was unable to go beyond a "new subsistence state" (Nixon 2012). By 1996, Tim-Tim was one of the poorest provinces of Indonesia, with its GDP at less than half the national average and with one third of households living in extreme poverty (more than twice the Indonesian average). The most relevant feature, though, was the very high level of repression exercised by the Indonesian authorities, which prevented the Timorese from "imagining" themselves as part of a new nation (Anderson 1993). On the contrary, they took advantage of increased schooling and Indonesia's official narrative of heroic dissent regarding their Dutch former masters to "imagine" themselves as the rebels against the new oppressors.

The independent Commission for Reception, Truth, and Reconciliation (CAVR in its Tetum/Portuguese acronym) set up under UN supervision drew dramatic conclusions. To start with, the number of deaths increased many fold over their expected levels, mainly in the years 1975–80. CAVR minimum estimates point to 102,800 deaths due to direct killings and indirect ones due to hunger and illness but admits that figures in the region of 200,000 are plausible (CAVR 2013). If one considers that the population of Portuguese Timor in 1975 was around 670,000, and that an average 150,00 deaths were reported, then one finds a situation that has a parallel in the Cambodian Killing Fields of the Khmer Rouge (1.7 to 2.5 million out of 8 million). The litany of non-fatal repression includes forced displacements, unlawful detention, torture, rape, sexual slavery and violence, forced marriage, impediments to reproductive rights, destruction of homes and livestock, extortion, forced recruitment and forced labor, and more. Scholars have debated the extent to which this sort of brutal repression over a defenseless people amounts to the notion of genocide. Clinton Fernandes (2023) has argued—in what seems a well reasoned argument—that it does indeed correspond to an attempted genocide. In his conclusion he is supported by respected members of the Catholic Church for whom the atrocities perpetrated in Tim-Tim amount to "cultural genocide."

In this context, resistance to Indonesian rule grew stronger with the passing of time. From a moment when it was centered around FRETILIN's "liberated areas" to the formation, in 1998, of the National Council of the Timorese Resistance bringing under a common umbrella a multitude of dissenters, the road was long. The Resistance comprised a military wing, namely a handful of guerrilla fighters that symbolically kept the flame alive; a diplomatic front acting abroad and conducting critical work in relation to governments and world public opinion; and an ever growing number of "clandestine" activists—in reality, a vast number of Timorese were dissatisfied with the regime, including the emerging students' movement that would be important in the last years of the occupation. To all this, one must add the contribution of the Timorese Catholic Church, a unifying factor that offered a solid reference base to the sense of national community and opposition to the occupiers.

The evolution of world politics also played a significant part in the developments of the 1990s. The demise of the Cold War brought to the fore a new narrative of respect of human rights—a field in which Indonesia was increasingly isolated, namely after the footage of the Santa Cruz Massacre (November 12, 1991) was broadcasted worldwide. At the UN, the election of Kofi Annan was also a significant boost to the "Timor issue," as the new Secretary General took it on himself to increase pressure for a negotiated settlement. Two years into his first term, Portugal and Indonesia signed an agreement under his aegis (May 5, 1999), and the way was open for the staging of a genuine act of self-determination.

On August 30, 1999 a "popular consultation" preceded by a comprehensive registration of voters took place in Timor-Leste. A total of 446,953 citizens registered to vote, of which 98.93 percent actually came to the polls. Indonesia's offer of a "special autonomy" within the republic was chosen by 94,388 people (21.5 percent), whereas the rejection of such an offer, which amounted to a choice for independence, received 344,580 votes (78.5 percent).

Right after the results were announced in New York, "hell descended on earth" (in the words of the UK representative at the UN, Sir Jeremy Greenstock, who visited Dili in early September). Local militias armed and backed by the Indonesian military pursued a scorched-earth policy, bringing to the ground much of the Indonesian legacy in terms of physical infrastructures and public administration. Under strong international pressure, Indonesian president B. J. Habibie accepted the deployment of INTERFET—International Force for East Timor—that brought a modicum of peace to a tormented territory. On

October 17, the Indonesian Parliament voted—355 to 322—to accept the results of the referendum, leading to their withdrawal from Timor-Leste. The UN was then prepared to create the United Nations Transitional Authority in East Timor (UNTAET—UN Resolution 1272[1999], October 25) and initiate the third and final moment of the long process of Timor-Leste self-determination.

UNTAET received a very comprehensive mandate—the "most powerful mission" in all of the UN's history of involvement in nation-building (Tansey 2009). The mission was headed by Brazilian-born UN diplomat Sérgio Vieira de Mello (who had previous experience in Kosovo), vested with extensive powers in order to—among others—"support capacity building for self-government." His powers comprised "the exercise of all legislative and executive authority, including the administration of justice." Many observers suggested this was a subtle way to express the desire for the installation of a Western liberal democracy template with little input from the Timorese. For this reason Vieira de Mello was compared to a "pre-constitutional monarch in a sovereign state" (Chopra) and the method to bring about a new democratic polity regarded as "benevolent autocracy" (Chesterman), "benevolent despotism" (Beauvais), or "benevolent dictatorship" (Powell). Kingsbury labeled the exercise as "benign colonialism" (see Feijó 2016 for references). There was a blatant contradiction between the stated goals and the chosen method.

In fact, Vieira de Mello showed some sensitivity to the Timorese claims to be an active part of the process. At the beginning, the process was conducted in New York by the UN Department of Peacekeeping Operations (DPKO), which used its own template: in post-conflict environments, treat the warring factions as equals and do not offer them positions in executive power—quite a distance from the experience of the UN Department of Political Affairs (DPA) that knew fairly well all the Timorese forces and was fully aware that a legitimate referendum had returned a sound victory to one of the parts. Following the lead from DPKO, UNTAET initially created a "National Consultative Council" with representatives of both sides and devoid of executive powers. Later on, it reformulated that body into a "National Council," increasing the representation of the pro-independence forces, but still devoid of executive prerogatives.

A middle of the ground solution was eventually found: to install a transitional government that included four Timorese (but had to report to Vieira de Mello for approval) and to call elections for a constitutional assembly tasked with elaboration of the new country's basic laws following a brief period during which the local political formations had to apply for formal registration as parties. This election was held two years after the referendum on August 30, 2001 and a reshuffle of the transitional government was implemented to mirror the election's outcome. In March 2002 the new constitution was approved by majority vote, as two parties combined to secure the necessary 60 percent of the parliamentarians' vote, most smaller parties voting against it. Following the terms of the constitution, elections for a new president were held on April 14, 2002. These were called "the friendly elections," as the two candidates expressed mutual respect, and one of them admitted he was only running to honor the process. The charismatic leader of the Resistance, Xanana Gusmão, won (82.7 percent) over the man who had been sworn in as the first President of the Republic on November 28, 1975—Francisco Xavier do Amaral (17.3 percent). Taking advantage of a very controversial provision of the electoral law, the constitutional assembly decided to turn itself into the first parliament of the novel state. Conditions were thus met for the proclamation of (the restoration of) independence on May 20, 2002. After twenty-eight long and turbulent years, the former Portuguese colony, later Indonesian "province" under a neocolonial regime, turned into the very first nation-state of the twenty-first century.

2.

After the internationally recognized independence, a narrative emerged akin to a "whig interpretation of history," in which all actors had seemingly performed in accordance with the ultimate goal of securing a genuine act of self-determination for Timor-Leste. This image is far from the truth. In fact, the years during which Timor-Leste struggled for its self-determination are marked by a plethora of developments, shifts in attitudes, and policy changes. Portugal is no exception: during the period of Indonesian occupation, the country experienced a bumpy trajectory and admitted several solutions to solve the "Timor issue."

For one, the constitution bestowed powers over state policy in regard to Timor-Leste (and Macau) both to the President of the Republic and the government. In a semi-presidential regime, this means that their respective positions need not be similar—and they were not, at least during the initial years. The foreign policy priorities were clearly set on securing accession to the then called European Economic Community—and this fact rendered Portugal vulnerable to strong pressures from EEC members who had close ties with Indonesia and wished to pursue commercial relations unhindered by diplomatic constraints. It would take several years and Portugal's full accession to EEC for internal politics to shift in favor of a principled stance that had often been sacrificed on the altar of convenience. Zélia Pereira brings us a survey of the years 1976 to 1991 and shows how and when Portuguese attitudes toward the Timorese struggle for self-determination evolved toward staunch support for a genuine act of self-determination and the rejection of intermediate solutions proposed by Indonesia. On the whole, this piece calls our attention to the need to have a more nuanced view of Portugal's attitude.

A critical factor in the success of the Timor-Leste struggle for self-determination was the mobilization of world public opinion in favor of the repressed nation. This became particularly evident after the demise of the Cold War, when an agenda of human rights imposed itself on the compromises with authoritarianism that marked the heyday of the previous period. Although one may regard the right to self-determination to be a human right, it may be argued that in the 1980s and 1990s the willingness to accept claims to self-determination had waned significantly. From its heyday in the 1950s and 1960s, self-determination was later regarded as having been mostly accomplished, only a handful of smaller territories still lacking its fulfillment. In parallel, the idea of self-determination was flourishing in new, unexpected quarters; that was the case with Scotland (within the UK) and Catalonia (within the Spanish state) (Sterio 2013; Miller 2020). But then, most of the classical territories were regarded as too small and weak to sustain real self-rule. Moreover, several Asian and African independences had had a negative impact on the idealism that sustained self-determination. Many of their leaders in the fight against colonialism had spoiled their records and prestige by becoming heads of corrupt, fractious, and often brutal regimes (Chatterjee 1993). Conditions were ripe for a different narrative to emerge: that was the case for the discourse on human rights in a broad perspective.

Amy Rothschild brings us her reflections on how the narrative on human rights articulates with anticolonialism and self-determination. She argues that, as from the 1980s, the Timorese Resistance began to employ the narrative on human rights, and to use novel channels at the United Nations, in an effort to appeal to Western powers and their public opinion, portraying the sufferance of the Timorese people as a result not only of an act of aggression in contradiction with international law, but also of the brutal methods employed to subjugate the entire population. The ultimate political goal (a genuine act of self-determination) was thus mediated by a nonpolitical but rather moral stance: to end the brutality of the occupation.

The mobilization of the world's public opinion was a critical weapon used by the Timorese Resistance. In this endeavor, the Timorese were supported by a myriad of solidarity organizations who took it on themselves to feed both public opinion and governmental authorities with updated information on the current situation in the territory and organized forms of political pressure on policy makers. One of the leading organizations was the UK-based TAPOL, originally set up in 1965 by an Indonesian expat Carmel Budiardjo, in defense of political prisoners in her country. By 1976, TAPOL had evolved into a broader organization and took on itself the task of disseminating information on Timor-Leste (namely through a regular bulletin, which is a precious source of social history) and organizing pressure activities on behalf of, and in cooperation with, the Timorese Resistance. TAPOL is the subject of Hannah Loney's piece in this dossier. Based primarily on its bulletin, the piece highlights the importance of the solidarity movement in general by means of a special case study that is put in a broad context. The author's acknowledged sympathy for the subject does not prevent her from offering a sober, objective analytical narrative.

A more complex case is that of Indonesia. The fate of Timor-Leste was, for long, closely associated with the survival of the authoritarian regime of the New Order. Pocut Hanifah—an Indonesian scholar that ventured in hitherto virgin territory as far as the relations between the Timorese Resistance and the opposition to Suharto is concerned—places her piece under the aegis of a quote by the Timorese charismatic leader Xanana Gusmão: "The struggle for democratic reform in Indonesia and the fight in Timor-Leste have different agendas but the same enemy." The importance of this statement is not the obvious (the existence of a common enemy) but rather the acknowledgement that there were "different agendas." In fact, for a substantial part of the opposition to the New Order, the "Timor issue" was a non-question—it had been solved for good. The importance of Pocut Hanifah's contribution is thus to show that the intertwinement between the Timorese claims and those of the Indonesian opposition came late (in the mid 1990s) and was significantly underpinned by the impact of some Timorese organizations, like the student RENETIL (active in Indonesian universities). Still, the critical association of the nationalist claims by the Timorese and the democratic agenda of Indonesians was far from perfect (and thus external pressure was a relevant factor in B. J. Habibie's decision to accept a UN-sponsored referendum).

Michael Leach brings us a piece on the evolving role of the Catholic Church. During the Portuguese colonial times, the Catholic Church was a pillar of the status quo, going as far as to provide the local representative to sit on the Portuguese parliament. When decolonization was set, the local Church sided with the conservative elements, loudly criticizing the "Marxist" and "atheist" FRETILIN. The bishop of Dili, D. José Joaquim Ribeiro, famously said he had regarded the Indonesian paratroops as "angels from heaven" coming to liberate Timor-Leste from "communism" —only to realize they were rather "demons from hell." In fact, the Indonesian occupying forces did not spare the Catholic Church in their rampage in December 1975. Soon the local Church, which had undergone a significant process of the "Timorization" of its cadres and was no longer dependent on European clergymen, became entangled with grassroots forms of resistance to the severe abuses of human rights (even if many European clergymen remained in Timor-Leste and engaged in active resistance to Indonesian atrocities). A new bishop, D. Carlos Filipe Ximenes Belo, stated that Indonesians were carrying out a "cultural genocide" of the population and stood on their side. As the national character of the local Church was asserting itself (including with clashes with the Indonesian hierarchy and even with an ambiguous Vatican wary of the fate of several million Indonesian Catholics), it became a pillar of the resistance to the occupation. In the international context, the Timorese Catholic Church provided a rallying point for solidarity and dismissed the notion that the Resistance was the feat of a handful of "radicals." Indeed, the Timorese Catholic Church combined the support for the struggle for self-determination with the keeping of a conservative agenda—more in line with what was happening in Poland than in Latin America's "liberation theology."

The fact that this special dossier on Timor-Leste contains collaboration from scholars from Australia, Indonesia, Portugal, and the USA is a modest testimony to the transnational character of the belated, long, and troubled process of self-determination for Timor-Leste.

REFERENCES

Alexandre, Valentim. 2017. *Contra o Vento. Portugal, o Império e a Maré Anticolonial.* Lisboa: Temas & Debates.

Anderson, Benedict. 1993. "Imagining East Timor." *Arena Magazine* 4 (April-May). ftp://english. hss.cmu.edu/english.server/cultural.theory/Anderson-Imagining%20East%20Timor.

Cardina, Miguel. 2020. "O Passado Colonial. Do trajeto histórico às configurações da memória." In *O Século XX Português,* edited by Fernando Rosas et al., 357–411. Lisboa: Tinta da China.

Cardoso, António Monteiro. 2007. *Timor na II Guerra Mundial: O diário do Tenente Pires.* Lisboa: CECHP/ISCTE.

CAVR (Comissão de Acoilhimento, Verdade e Reconciliação). 2013. *Chega! The Final Report of the Timor-Leste Commission for Reception, Truth, and Reconciliation.* Jakarta: KPG in cooperation with STP/CAVR.

Chatterjee, Partha. 1993. *The Nation and Its Fragments. Colonial and Postcolonial Histories.* Princeton: Princeton University Press.

Durand, Frédéric. 2011. "Trois siècles de violence et de lutes au Timor oriental (1726-2008)." https://www.sciencespo.fr/mass-violence-war-massacre-resistance/fr/document/trois -siacles-de-violences-et-de-luttes-au-timor-oriental-1726-2008.html.

Feijó, Rui Graça. 2016. *Dynamics of Democracy in Timor-Leste. The Birth of a Democratic Nation.* Amsterdam: Amsterdam University Press.

___. 2022. "Os bastidores da Lei de Descolonização de Timor. Interacção entre Portugal e os movimentos nacionalistas timorenses." *Ler História* 80: 17–40.

Fernandes, Clinton. 2023. "The Indonesian Genocide in Timor-Leste: Law, Politics, History." In *Timor-Leste's Long Road to Independence. Transnational Perspectives*, edited by Zélia Pereira and Rui Graça Feijó, xxx-xxx. Amsterdam: Amsterdam University Press.

Jerónimo, Miguel Bandeira. 2018. "Repressive Developmentalism. Idioms, Repertoires and Trajectories in Late Colonialism." In *The Oxford Handbook of the Ends of Empires*, edited by Martin Thomas and Andrew S. Thompson, 537–54. Oxford: Oxford University Press.

Kammen, Douglas. 2016. *Three Centuries of Conflict in East Timor.* Singapore: National University of Singapore Press.

Miller, David. 2020. *Is Self-Determination a Dangerous Illusion?* Cambridge: Polity.

Nixon, Rod. 2012. *Justice and Governance in East Timor: Indigenous Approaches to the "New Subsistence State."* London: Routledge.

Pélissier, René. 1996. *Timor en Guerre. Le crocodile et les portugais (1847–1913).* Orgéval: Editions Pélissier.

Pereira, Zélia, and Rui Graça Feijó. 2022. "Portugal e a descolonização de Timor. Da Conferência de Macau à invasão indonésia." *Relações Internacionais* 74: 35–53

___. 2023. "Decolonisation without Self-Determination? Portuguese Perspectives on Indonesia's Involvement with Timor (1974–1975")." Bijdragen tot de taal-, land- en volkenkunde 179 (2): xxx-yyy

Santos, Aurora Almada, and Zélia Pereira. 2022. "Portugal, as Nações Unidas e a autodeterminação de Timor-Leste, 1974–1982." *Ler História* 80: 65–89.

Sterio, Milena. 2013. *The Right to Self-Determination under International Law.* London: Routledge.

Tansey, Oisín. 2009. *Regime Building. Democratization and International Administration.* Oxford: Oxford University Press.

Reality Overlapping Principles? Portugal and the Self-Determination of Timor-Leste (1976–91)

Zélia Pereira

Introduction

The history of Timor-Leste between the end of Portuguese colonialism (1975) and the moment it acceded internationally recognized independence (2002) is the subject of several academic studies as well as interventions by authors who participated or witnessed events both in its territory or in the international arena, shedding light on the Portuguese "unfinished decolonization."[1] The Indonesian occupation has attracted the attention of numerous authors, extending into the period following the UN-sponsored referendum of August 30, 1999 and focusing on human rights and the construction of

Zelia Pereira is Associate Researcher at the Institute for Contemporary History, NOVA University of Lisboa, and Senior Archivist at Mario Soares and Maria Barroso Foundation (Lisboa).

[1] This term was used by Fernando Figueiredo, "Da descolonização inacabada ao limiar da independência," *Povos e Culturas* 19 (2015): 275–98. There are several analyses of the events of 1974–75, including Moisés Silva Fernandes, "A Preponderância dos Factores Exógenos na Rejeição do Plano Português de Descolonização para Timor-Leste,1974–1975," *Negócios Estrangeiros* 10 (2007): 90–171; Rui Graça Feijó, ed., *Timor-Leste: Colonialismo, Descolonização, Lusutopia* (Porto: Afrontamento, 2016); or David Hicks, *Rhetoric and the Decolonization and Recolonization of East Timor* (New York: Routledge, 2015). Detailed information on these years is also provided by António Barbedo de Magalhães, *Timor-Leste: interesses internacionais e actores locais* (Porto: Afrontamento, 2007). Memoirs of actors in the process can be found in the book of the last governor, Colonel Mário Lemos Pires, *Timor: Missão Impossível* (Lisboa: Dom Quixote, 1991) and that of the minister in charge of decolonization, António de Almeida Santos, *Quase Memórias* (Cruz Quebrada: Casa das Letras, 2006).

the new nation.[2] The Timorese Resistance, both its internal—armed or clandestine—and external fronts, are referred in plenty of different sources: analytical, biographical, or memoirs.[3] Finally, the international dimension of the Timor-Leste question has been discussed in numerous publications, considering the positions of several countries, the United Nations, or the contribution of solidarity movements.[4]

However, there is still much to learn about the history of the attitudes of Indonesia and Portugal on the Timor-Leste question and the policies these countries pursued after the invasion.[5] The present essay aims to mitigate these lacunae by focusing on the case of Portugal based on the increasingly available archival material. In the following sections, the hesitations that marred Portuguese attitudes after 1976, the constant infighting between the defense of principles and the acceptance of harsh reality, and the weak capacity to counter the status quo will be highlighted. It will be revealed how, contrary to the current image of national unity and broad consensus regarding Timor-Leste and its struggle for self-determination, the Portuguese organs of sovereignty rarely had a unanimous position, and the main political leaders competed to set priorities and to make strategic options.

The methodological approach for the analysis presented in these pages is based mainly on primary sources deriving from extensive archival research in untapped archives in Portugal. We hope to provide a valuable contribution in making Portuguese-language diplomatic documents from the archives available to an English-speaking readership. However it must be noted that legal restrictions still apply to numerous documents under secrecy rules or covered by the "thirty years" principle of confidentiality, hence the

---

[2] See, among others, Matthew Jardine, *East Timor: Genocide in Paradise* (Tucson: Odonian Press, 1995); John G. Taylor, *East Timor: The Price of Freedom* (New York: Zed Books, 1999); James Dunn, *East Timor: A Rough Passage to Independence* (Double Bay, AUS: Longueville Books, 2003); Elizabeth Stanley, *Torture, Truth and Justice: The Case of Timor-Leste* (London: Routledge, 2009); Joseph Nevins, *A Not-So-Distant Horror: Mass Violence in East Timor* (Ithaca: Cornell University Press, 2005); Damien Kingsbury, *East Timor: The Price of Liberty* (New York: Palgrave-Macmillan, 2009); Michael Leach, *Nation-Building and National Identity in Timor-Leste* (New York: Routledge, 2017).

[3] Special mention must be given to the extensive information contained in the report of CAVR—Commission for Reception, Truth, and Reconciliation, *Chega!* (Jakarta: KPG in cooperation with STP-CAVR, 2013). Narratives on the Resistance and biographies include José Ramos-Horta, *Funu, the Unfinished Saga of East Timor* (Trenton: The Red Sea Press: 1987); José Ramos-Horta, *Timor Leste: amanhã em Díli* (Lisboa: Dom Quixote, 1994); Rowena Lennox, *Fighting Spirit of East Timor: The Life of Martinho da Costa Lopes* (London: Zed Books, 2000); E. Rees, "Under Pressure: FALINTIL—Forças de Defesa de Timor-Leste, Three Decades of Defence Force Development in Timor-Leste, 1975-2004," DCAF Working Paper no.139 (Geneva: Geneva Centre for the Democratic Control of Armed Forces, 2004); José Mattoso, *A Dignidade. Konis Santana e a Resistência Timorense* (Rio de Mouro: Círculo de Leitores/Fundação Mário Soares, 2005); Mário Viegas Carrascalão, *Timor antes do futuro* (Dili: Mau Huran Printing, 2006); Naldo Rei, *Resistance: A Childhood Fighting for East Timor* (St Lucia, AUS: University of Queensland Press, 2007); Sarah Niner, *Xanana* (Alfragide: Dom Quixote, 2011).

[4] See among others, Clinton Fernandes, *Independence of East Timor: Multi-Dimensional Perspectives—Occupation, Resistance, & International Political Activism* (Brighton: The Sussex Library of Asian Studies 2011); Peter Carey (with Pat Walsh), "The Security Council and East Timor," in *The Security Council and War*, ed. Vaughan Lowe, Adam Roberts, Jennifer Walsh, and Dominik Zaum (Oxford: OUP, 2008).

[5] For the case of Indonesia, on which there are scant contributions, see Mubyarto et al., *East Timor, the Impact of Integration: An Indonesian Socio-Anthropological Study* (Northcote, AUS: Indonesia Resources and Information Program, 1991); Frédéric Durand and Stéphane Dovert, "Crónica de uma anexação hesitante: a invasão do Timor Português pela Indonésia, 1974–1976," in Rui Graça Feijó, *Timor-Leste*, 329–51; as well as the memoirs of Indonesian diplomat and minister Ali Alatas, *The Pebble in the Shoe. The Diplomatic Struggle for East Timor* (Jacarta: Aksara Karunia, 2006).

decision to bring the study up to 1991 and not proceed to a period under considerable difficulties for accessing material. This decision is further sustained by the belief that 1991, and the impact of the Santa Cruz Massacre, marked a turning point in the Portuguese attitude toward Timor-Leste. Also for the post-1991 period, there is extensive literature and more work available regarding Portugal's position, but the previous years are in many ways more revealing in overturning a view of a benevolent and always activist Portugal.

Portugal Reacts to Indonesian Annexation

After the fall of the authoritarian regime on April 25, 1974, the Portuguese authorities embarked on a complex decolonizing process that would lead to the independence of all its African colonies. Timor-Leste did not assume a prominent place in this process, in part due to the fact that no war was ravaging its territory nor had it any liberation movement internationally recognized, but still it fell under the rules set by Law 7/74 (July 27) that granted all colonies the right to self-determination and independence.

In September 1974, Foreign Minister (MNE) Mário Soares declared before the UN General Assembly (UNGA) that Portugal would consult with the Timorese to ascertain their preferences regarding their future. Even though doubts surfaced on the viability of an independent state and the possibility was raised of the integration of the half-island into its neighbor Indonesia, for the Portuguese authorities the principle of a consultation was both politically and ethically mandatory and a condition for any solution. In the contacts established with the Indonesian authorities in 1974–75, this was always a non-negotiable principle, while guarantees that Indonesian interests would be considered were also on the table.[6] Negotiations conducted with the Timorese nationalist movements that emerged after April 25, 1974, were also driven toward guaranteeing that, whatever the final outcome would be, a popular consultation was a requirement for decolonization. Law 7/75 (July 17) was approved after complex and difficult conversations with the three main movements and established a roadmap for the self-determination process "in accordance with the pertinent UN resolutions."[7] Its cornerstone was the election by free, universal, and secret ballot of an assembly tasked with deciding which way to proceed "in tune with the genuine will of the Timorese people."

The civil war that engulfed the territory in August 1975 took place at a time when Portugal was facing severe internal strife, and the provisions of Law 7/75 could not be implemented. In spite of the efforts of the Portuguese authorities to bring the opposing sides to the negotiation table, and the difficult dialogue with Indonesia, it was not possible to scale down tension and events evolved till the Indonesian invasion on December 7, 1975.[8] Portugal pressed charges with the UN Security Council. The UNSC resolutions, as well as the General Assembly's, called for the deployment of a fact-finding mission, which was eventually sent under Vittorio Winspeare Guicciardi as UNSG special envoy.

---

[6] See Zélia Pereira and Rui Graça Feijó, "Decolonization without self-determination? Portuguese perspectives on Indonesia's involvement with Timor (1974–1975)", *Bijdragen tot de Taal-, Land- en Volkenkunde* (2023, forthcoming).

[7] Rui Graça Feijó, "Os bastidores da Lei de Descolonização de Timor. Interação entre Portugal e os movimentos nacionalistas timorenses," *Ler História* 80 (2022): 17–40.

[8] Zélia Pereira and Rui Graça Feijó, "Portugal e a descolonização de Timor. Da Cimeira de Macau à invasão indonésia," *Revista R:I* 74 (2022): 35–53.

In subsequent months, Portugal witnessed events unfolding while keeping some navy vessels in the vicinity of Timor. At the same time, Portugal developed mostly secretive contacts with Indonesia in order to release a group of military personnel held in custody since the end of the civil war. Guicciardi's visit in February 1976 produced scant results: he was unable to meet with FRETILIN personnel in the territory and could not secure the release of the prisoners. After he submitted his report, the UNSC met again to discuss this issue in April 1976. The new resolution did not influence the course of action: Indonesia did not back up, but rather tried to offer its move a legitimizing face—it convened a "Popular Assembly" (May 31) composed of chosen elements who approved a petition to President Suharto asking for Timor-Leste to be integrated into Indonesia, a move that was sanctioned by the Parliament on July 17. Timor-Leste was henceforth considered as Indonesia's 27th Province.

Few options were left to Portugal to criticize Indonesia and support the Timorese's rights to self-determination other than insisting on UN initiatives. Diplomat Costa Lobo, chargé d'affaires of the Permanent Mission of Portugal to the United Nations, would sum up before the Committee of 24[9] (September 1976) its position: Portugal would not recognize the integration of Timor-Leste into Indonesia "not because it opposes such a possibility," but because the process was not conducted in a fair manner and did not respect the people's will. Portugal would continue to claim its position as "administering power of a non-autonomous territory"—a position that was grounded in UN procedures—and considered that the issue was now completely in the hands of the UN as a problem that did not derive from a bilateral conflict between Portugal and Indonesia, but was, in fact, a question of the international community's responsibility.[10]

1976–81: Facing Reality, Questioning Strategies

In the years following the annexation of Timor-Leste, Portugal based its strategy on the same principles that had guided its decolonization process, assuming the right to self-determination as a legal and moral imperative. Principles granted by the United Nations Charter and General Assembly resolutions provided the bases for the international juridical framework to justify the right of Timor-Leste's people to self-determination. UNGA Resolutions 1514 and 1541 (both of 1960) were paramount as they regarded the right of colonized peoples to independence and established the principles on which member states were obliged to provide the UN with information on the non-autonomous territories under their jurisdiction[11]—Timor-Leste being in the list of Portugal's dependent

---

[9] The Committee of 24 was the designation of the Special Committee on the Situation with Regard to the Implementation of the Declaration on the Granting of Independence to Colonial Countries and Peoples. It was a special committee of the UN General Assembly established in 1961 exclusively devoted to the issue of decolonization.

[10] A. Costa Lobo, "As coordenadas da posição de Portugal em relação a Timor (Projeto de definição de posição elaborado em 13-08-1976 na Missão Permanente de Portugal junto das Nações Unidas)," August 18, 1976, Arquivo Histórico Diplomático/Ministério dos Negócios Estrangeiros (AHD/MNE), PAA 1456.

[11] The Resolution 1514 (XV), December 14, 1960, known as the Declaration on the Granting of Independence to Colonial Countries and Peoples recognized the right of every people under foreign domination the right to self-determination and to freely decide on their political status. The Resolution 1541 (XV), December 15, 1960, clarified the terms of Article 73 of the UN Charter in connection with the member states' obligation to convey information on their non-autonomous territories and making clear the possible formulae to obtain self-rule: independence, free association with an independent nation, or the integration into an independent state.

territories. One might add new resolutions approved by the UNGA in December 1975 as well as those of the UNSC in December 1975 and April 1976. Portugal insisted on its acceptance of all the UN resolutions, refusing to concede on the issue of Indonesia's annexation, and claiming its status as administering power in accordance with Chapter XI of the UN Charter.[12]

On the internal front, the approval of the Constitution of the Portuguese Republic (April 2, 1976) represented a sound juridical piece in the process. Not only did it recognize the right of peoples to self-determination and independence as the basic principle of its relations with the international community (Section 7), but it included a specific section (307) on the "independence of Timor," which reads:

1. Portugal remains committed to the responsibilities that fall upon it, in accordance with international law, to promote and guarantee the right of Timor-Leste to independence.

2. It is incumbent upon the President of the Republic, assisted by the Council of the Revolution, and upon the Government to carry all the necessary actions required to fulfil the above stipulation.

As far as non-juridical principles are concerned, one must stress the moral obligation Portugal had toward the people of its former colony. First of all, there was an issue of national pride and honor derived from the failed attempt to secure peaceful decolonization, which called for a moral commitment to secure self-determination. In the context of national politics, the Timor question was shrouded in polemics and involved suspicion on the performance of political and military leaders, sometimes threatening the still-fragile democracy. As for Timor itself, news arrived regularly in Lisboa reporting the resistance to the invaders and the atrocities they were perpetrating. Portugal could not help but face its responsibilities, as the solidarity movements were growing and taking hold of public opinion.

Once the question was firmly in UN hands, Portugal assumed a low-profile attitude, deciding not to cosponsor resolution proposals that were mostly penned by José Ramos-Horta, FRETILIN leading representative, and that were subscribed by the former Portuguese colonies in Africa—but voting in favor of their approval. However, the main thrust was not to openly antagonize Indonesia; not to claim any special authority on a matter regarded as pertaining to the realm of the relations between Indonesia and the entire international community, not a bilateral issue with Portugal; and to accept any outcome that would guarantee respect for the main principles involved. There was an implicit assumption: Portugal wanted to keep room for maneuvers that might allow it to unilaterally declare its responsibilities as administering power as extinct given the de facto situation. The idea that the annexation was "irreversible" was shared by some Portuguese diplomats even when Portugal voted in favor of the resolution approved at the UNGA in 1976.[13] That idea gained roots among the Portuguese authorities

---

[12] Every year since 1976, the Portuguese representative at the UN, following on the stipulations of Resolution 1541, addressed the UNSG a formal letter explaining why it was not possible for Portugal to comply with that resolution given the situation created by the Indonesian annexation, thus fulfilling its formal duties as administering power.

[13] Quartin Santos report, Portuguese mission at UN, December 22, 1976, AHD/MNE, PAA 1456.

who believed that the right attitude was not to antagonize Indonesia and thus create conditions for some kind of dialogue with Jakarta.[14]

Portugal assumed a passive attitude, refraining from raising the issue other than when it was discussed by virtue of someone else's initiatives, and lacking firm purposes, support for the Timor cause was slowly losing its initial appeal. Every year, the number of votes in favor was dwindling in the UNGA. The same happened in the Non-Aligned Movement, being increasingly difficult to insert any mention of Timor in its communiqués. On the contrary, support for Indonesia's stance grew steadily, coming from important quarters, such as the USA, Japan, Canada, or Australia, who had the capacity to influence other nations. Even at a time when alarming news spread around mentioning severe food shortages and hunger waves in 1979, Jakarta—aware that human rights could herald a new phase in international criticism—presented the problem as stemming from FRETILIN's struggle, the shallow development of the territory under Portuguese colonial domination, and boasted about investments recently made.[15]

The Portuguese Mission at the UN provided Lisboa with frequent reports urging a change of orientation. In 1978, Filipe Albuquerque sent the proposed resolution project for the 33rd UNGA, penned by FRETILIN, and suggested that Portugal should "ponder the possibility of changing its stance," having in mind that "the absence of a final negotiated settlement was detrimental of the possibility of establishing relations with Indonesia" and that it was mandatory to resume negotiations with Jakarta "before the international community—either by inertia or by deliberation—ratifies the current situation."[16] The following year, Ambassador Vasco Futscher Pereira would support the need for Portugal to revise its position as the country was increasingly marginalized in this respect and unable to counter the growing support that Indonesia was conquering:

> We can hardly maintain without grave harm—both internally and externally—the strategy we have been following, consisting of recognizing the Portuguese incapacity to uphold its duties as administering power, and voting in the UN for resolutions that condemn Indonesia. . . . It seems that the current situation, which does not satisfy FRETILIN nor the countries that support it, and does not contribute to bringing Portugal and Indonesia closer together, does not serve the national interest. . . . Having in mind political, human and cultural interests and the importance of Indonesia in the international context, it would be convenient

---

[14] This sort of approach was implemented in 1979–80 when Portugal was elected to a place in the UNSC. In those two years, Portugal—who still had a pending complaint since 1975—decided not to use its position to raise the issue. In March 1978, when the candidacy was being prepared, Ambassador Vasco Futscher Pereira suggested to the Foreign Minister that contacts should be made with Indonesia to prevent the country from opposing the idea, insisting that a "dropped word" might be useful to convey that "Portugal has no intention to raise the issue of Timor at the UN, let alone in the UNSC" in case the election was secured. Telegram 165, Mission at UN to MNE, March 28, 1978, AHD/MNE, PAA 1456.

[15] About the issue of Timor-Leste at the UN and Portugal's low-profile attitude, see Aurora Almada e Santos and Zélia Pereira, "Portugal, as Nações Unidas e a autodeterminação de Timor-Leste, 1974–1982," *Ler História* 80 (2022): 65–89; and Zélia Pereira *"Damned if You Do, Damned if You Don't*. Portugal, the UN and the Timor-Leste Issue," in *Timor-Leste's Long Road to Independence. Transnational Perspectives*, ed. Zélia Pereira and Rui Graça Feijó (Amsterdam: AUP, 2023).

[16] Letter 1005, Filipe Albuquerque, Mission at UN to MNE, June 30, 1978, AHD/MNE, PAA 1456.

to unlock the situation, by means of resuming previous contacts, framing them conveniently, in the first phase, in humanitarian concerns.[17]

A memo produced at the Foreign Ministry toward the end of 1979 concluded that it seemed unlikely that the UN—"lacking the means or the will"—would find a way out of the question. Portugal should not "expect that Indonesia, acting as a repentant thief, would one day return what it had unlawfully appropriated."[18] Indonesia was fully aware of its prestige within the Non-Aligned Movement and its position in a sensitive geopolitical area and expected the eventual reluctance of Western countries would decrease by means of natural erosion. In this light, Jakarta invested in upgrading its image, inviting foreign diplomats and the International Committee of the Red Cross (ICRC) to visit Timor-Leste. FRETILIN, militarily weakened, did not seem to represent a real threat.

Portugal had to make choices. The first option was to keep its position unchanged. That would be comfortable and would not burden its policies: Portugal would maintain a "juridical fiction," to proclaim its sovereignty over Timor-Leste, to condemn Indonesia, and to reveal, every now and then, humanitarian concerns. However, the "usual verbalism" at the UN could elicit criticism for its passivity and would not respond to the Timorese nationalist movements, thus feeding resentment without any practical advantage.

A second option would consist of a more dynamic intervention at the UN and other international fora. This would imply presenting their own resolutions at the UN, or seconding initiatives from countries that were more openly against Indonesia and presented more aggressive proposals. In limine, this could lead to Portugal seconding initiatives undertaken by FRETILIN. In other fora, this option included sponsoring or supporting verbal attacks on Indonesia in the media, or to develop more aggressive initiatives directed at friendly countries with a view to beef up their support for Timor-Leste, eventually to FRETILIN itself. This option contained higher risks, as it would represent a change of attitude without any guarantees of success. According to the memo, it was unrealistic to suppose that certain countries would "sacrifice their own interests in the altar of foreign causes." Also, this course of action might jeopardize any future attempt to approximate Indonesia.

A third option was the recognition of Indonesian annexation. This would allow Portugal to solve several problems—for instance, the high cost involved in the repatriation of Timorese who fled to Lisboa—but had severe setbacks. Even though Portugal had decolonized the African territories, Timor-Leste was still very present in the national public opinion that was not ready to accept "a hasty recognition of the occupation." Externally, some would become satisfied by the disappearance of a frictional issue, but others—in particular, the former Portuguese colonies—would condemn the move and provoke negative consequences for the bilateral relations being established. In sum: Portugal would meet Indonesian interests without any gain.

---

[17] Telegram 414, Futscher Pereira, Mission at UN to MNE, June 5, 1979, ADH/MNE, S16/E79/P02/90346.

[18] Non-signed memorandum, MNE, December 20, 1979: "Portugal e a questão de Timor-Leste," AHD/MNE, S16/E79/P02/90346.

Considering the pros and cons of these three options, a fourth one emerged: the gradual unlocking of the question. Overture and dialogue would be avenues to explore in line with a program determining the right occasion for and the level at which contacts should be established. The approximation to dialogue with Indonesia ought to be resumed as soon as possible given the dramatic situation in the territory and the international aid that was flowing through IRC with Jakarta's consent. The suggestion was made that the first approach should emphasize the humanitarian dimension in order to dispel criticism from the national public opinion. It would not imply a substantial change of position, nor the need to reestablish diplomatic relations with Indonesia. It would be no more than an interim solution.

In January 1980, the new VI Constitutional Government was sworn in and decided to revise the Portuguese position on this matter, assuming a renewed interest in the promotion of Timor-Leste's right to self-determination through new efforts to unlock the issue.[19] Constitutionally, the responsibility for the political decisions regarding Timor-Leste pertained to both the President of the Republic (PR) and the government, but the new Prime Minister (PM), Francisco Sá Carneiro, decided to call on himself the main role in foreign policy running against the president, who claimed his right to have a decisive word. Timor-Leste contributed to the climate of high tension between the president and the government.[20] The president reacted to this stance by convening a meeting of the Council of the Revolution (CR), focusing his point of view on the need to maintain "institutional solidarity" and considering that any initiative should be agreed on by both organs of sovereignty. The councilors were not unanimous in their appreciation of the theoretical issue but were agreed on its implications for Timor, the conviction being generalized that there were no conditions for Portugal to alter the situation in the territory. A special commission working inside the CR concluded that the situation in Timor-Leste was "irreversible" and acknowledged that "without new political facts" it would be "virtually impossible to obtain renewed conditions to allow for Portugal to resume the effective exercise of its responsibilities as administering power." The way ahead should be grounded in contacts with Indonesia in the framework of the UN, with a view to unlock gradually the situation and allow for a formula to emerge that would safeguard the interests of all parties.[21] Hard reality was undisputable. Only the strategy to obtain the stated goals could be questioned.

Both the government and the presidency reviewed the methodology and the content of the proposed initiatives leading to the desired dialogue with Indonesia. Divergences between PR and PM, reflecting an internal political conjuncture of open competition, meant that decisions were delayed. However, both politicians concurred that the need was felt to find a solution adapted to the circumstances.

---

[19] It was a coalition government of the Democratic Alliance (AD-Aliança Democrática), a center-right conservative political alliance, between the Social Democratic Party (PPD/PSD), the Democratic and Social Centre (CDS), and the People's Monarchist Party (PPM). Before this, only the II and IV Constitutional Governments programs contained brief references to the Timor issue.

[20] On the difficult relations between president and government, see Francisco Pinto Balsemão, *Memórias* (Lisboa: Porto Editora, 2021). The correspondence between Eanes and Sá Carneiro on the theme of Timor is kept at Ephemera—Private Library and Archive of José Pacheco Pereira.

[21] Minutes of CR meetings, January 16 and 23, 1980, and memo by the CR special commission, "O Problema de Timor," annex to the minutes of 23-01, Fundação Mário Soares e Maria Boarroso (Mário Soares and Maria Barroso Foundation), Conselho da Revolução (Council of the Revolution), docs. 02975.234 e 02975.235.

From New York, Ambassador Futscher Pereira advised the government to adopt a realistic stance:

> In the period immediately before the Indonesian military intervention, Portugal discharged wrongly its duties. At present, no matter how hard it is to face it, Timor is integrated into Indonesia and under these circumstances there is only one way to try and fulfil the moral solidarity duties derived from the historical ties that unite Portugal to the Timorese people—one must seek to negotiate with Indonesia conditions for those to be exercised.[22]

In Lisboa, the jurist Crucho de Almeida analyzed all the possible forms to frame the legal concept of self-determination and the limits Portugal faced to recognize Indonesian sovereignty over Timor. He concluded in support of what Futscher Pereira had hinted: "it is not viable to obtain from Indonesia an agreement to organize a referendum or even a consultation of elected officials under UN supervision." However, should Portugal "recognize the annexation without a legitimizing support from the UN, it would risk being exposed to criticism for its action would be no more than a withdrawal before a *fait accompli*." At the same time, he considered that "an eventual unlocking of this issue cannot avoid its re-appreciation by the UN, a situation that would raise the issue of how to unleash the process, and the significant factual bases for it to happen."[23]

At the UN, the Portuguese mission tried to approach informally the Indonesian delegation. On July 31, MNE Freitas do Amaral sent specific instructions to the ambassador in view of obtaining an agreement for a secret meeting with the Indonesian counterpart after he had been tipped that Indonesia, via the Netherlands, had suggested starting bilateral negotiations to consider a "hypothesis to be further analyzed": to use the 1982 legislative election in Indonesia to test the self-determination of Timor.[24] The government had a plan of action in mind, but it did not wish to present it to the PR before it had been tested in an informal conversation with the Indonesian ambassador at the UN. In order not to yield the idea that Portugal was "going to speak with Indonesia," it should be made clear that the meeting was merely destined to "exchange ideas" and organize it in such a way as to coincide with other meetings Portugal was engaging with FRETILIN and the former African colonies.[25]

Early in September 1980, Futscher Pereira had the opportunity to talk to the Indonesian Foreign Minister in New York. Mochtar Kusumaatmadja stressed that Indonesia had only acted on Timor when confronted with the "abandonment" of Portugal and could not backtrack. He wished Portugal and the international community "in a realistic way" decided to recognize the extant situation.[26] Meanwhile, rumors were spread that Indonesia was trying to delay the debate on the Timor issue at the UNGA, and this was interpreted by Portugal as a conciliatory gesture.[27]

---

[22] Memorandum, Futscher Pereira to MNE, April 24, 1980, AHD/MNE, Futscher Pereira archive, S012/UI043.

[23] Advice, Crucho de Almeida, "O caso de Timor-Leste," April, 15, 1980, AHD/MNE, S16/E79/P02/90346.

[24] Instructions, MNE to ambassador at the UN, July 31, 1980, AHD/MNE, S16/E79/P02/90346.

[25] Instructions, MNE to ambassador at the UN, August 25, 1980, AHD/MNE, S16/E79/P02/90346.

[26] Telegrams 575-576, Mission at UN to MNE, September 4, 1989, AHD/MNE, PAA 136.

[27] Telegram 600 Mission at UN to MNE, September, 8, 1989, AHD/MNE, Futscher Pereira archive, S012/UI043.

On September 12, a press release of the Portuguese government presented the decision to initiate consultations on the future of Timor, involving the parliamentary parties and "representative movements" of the Timorese people, and to develop more incisive diplomatic efforts. In parallel, it made public a plan to support Timorese refugees in Portugal, both on economic and humanitarian bases, and proposed to entertain conversations with Indonesia on these matters.[28] The president reacted again, censoring the government. If the plan to help the refugees garnered his support, the consultation process was outside the constitutional boundaries, as every phase of the process should include the active participation of the head of state.[29] Once again, an institutional quarrel weakened the position of Portugal, and not even the change of government in January 1981 would alter the situation.

The expectations on the dialogue with Indonesia were not met. Indonesia did not respond to the Portuguese challenge and the idea of using the diplomatic avenue to negotiate was even obfuscated in the international arena by reports in early 1981 that the Portuguese authorities were making it difficult for the Timorese refugees to obtain their passports. In March, the new PM, Francisco Pinto Balsemão, and MNE André Gonçalves Pereira discussed with their Dutch counterparts the Portuguese position and sought intermediation for a meeting with Indonesia.[30] In New York, Gonçalves Pereira would meet the UNSG on March 26 and propose the creation of an international commission under his good offices, assuming that Portugal would abide by its recommendations. He had in mind withdrawing the issue from the UNGA agenda. This item was raised once again when Kurt Waldheim visited Lisboa in May.[31]

After many contacts, it was not before September 1981 that an informal meeting took place in The Hague. On the side of Portugal, the diplomat Matos Proença was present. He met the minister councilor of the Indonesian embassy in Paris, Wisser Loeis, who claimed to be there only to take notes, as his mandate allowed simply "to limit himself to hear and transmit what Portugal had to say." The Indonesian diplomat seemed interested to ascertain whether a positive attitude on the part of his country would have positive effects on the Portuguese strategy at the UN.[32] The UNGA had started its session not long before, and Indonesia was keen to evaluate the situation before making any move. The pretext for the Indonesian silence regarding the Portuguese initiatives was the speech of the MNE at the UNGA. Mochtar Kusumaatmadja would later complain to the UNSG that the Portuguese minister had said that "nothing happened," keeping a high tone in his public statements.[33] The Indonesian minister excused himself to discuss the politics of the issue in his meeting with the UNSG, and Waldheim transmitted to the Portuguese minister that without an agreement between the parts he could not proceed with his own diligences, including the creation of the proposed commission.

---

[28] Press release, Council of Ministers, September 12, 1980, AHD/MNE, S16/E79/P02/90346.

[29] Letter, PR to PM, October 2, 1980, Arquivo Histórico da Presidência da República (AHPR), CC0210/3748.

[30] Report on the MNE conversation, annex to letter 170, MNE to Mission at the UN, March 11, 1981, AHD/MNE, Futscher Pereira archive, S012/UI043.

[31] Reports of the UNSG meetings of March 26, 1981 and May 9, 1981, UN Archives, SG Kurt Waldheim, S-0904-0087-0016-00001 UC.

[32] Telegram 188, Matos Proença to MNE, September 22, 1981, AHPR, CC0210/3747.

[33] Report of the UNSG meeting with Portuguese MNE, September 29, 1981, UN Archives, SG Kurt Waldheim, S-0904-0087-0016-00001 UC.

For Portugal, this meant having to declare publicly that all means to achieve a dialogue had been exhausted.[34] When the UNGA session closed, PM Pinto Balsemão informed the president that the government's political and diplomatic efforts initiated after September 1980 were terminated. He also referred that, from that moment onward, the president had to assume higher responsibilities under the constitution.[35]

1982–85: exploring the alternatives, negotiating with Indonesia

With the Timor issue back in his hands, President Eanes convened the CR. The councilors thought it necessary to engage in a different strategy in order to contravene the time factor playing in Indonesia's favor and called for a more intense course of actions in view of showing the country's commitment to a peaceful solution. At the internal level, the proposal was made to involve the political parties and especially the Parliament to foster the emergence of a national consensus. As for the international arena, the idea was to launch a joint action of the PR and the government in view of engaging a negotiating process with Indonesia based on humanitarian grounds. Recognition of FRETILIN as the sole representative of the Timorese people was mentioned but dismissed not to hamper relations with Indonesia.

The president translated the need for a new impetus by appointing Maria de Lourdes Pintasilgo as Special Councilor for the Timor issue.[36] Pintasilgo responded by intensifying internal and external contacts in order to find a new solution and to seek support for the Portuguese position. Under her guidance, numerous contacts would be developed with NGOs, activists, journalists, foreign personalities associated with the Catholic Church, and solidarity movements with human rights agendas. The foreign policy pursued by the government and the diplomats in key posts was actively accompanied. Another important aspect of her tenure was the establishment of regular contacts with representatives of Timorese nationalist movements, namely with FRETILIN, as well as with the special commission created in the Parliament (April 1982) to deal with the situation in the territory.

Portugal remained legally bound to promote and guarantee Timor's right to independence, even though pragmatic alternatives had to be sought. Considering the issue was losing prominence in the international arena, and that it might be withdrawn from the UNGA agenda—a defeat for Portugal and a serious obstacle to further positive steps—the delineated strategy at the presidency had two goals in mind: to safeguard legal and moral principles and postpone the recognition of the annexation, gaining time for a new solution to emerge. It comprehended two plans. First, on a social and humanitarian dimension, it aimed at providing a response to the pressing needs of the Timorese refugees (leaving the territory, family reunions, and assistance to those who were already in Lisboa) and to lay the bases for a debate on the violation of human rights to be held at the UN Human Rights Committee (HRC). The second plan was political and consisted of keeping the Timor issue alive at the UN by other means than

[34] Telegram 447, Mission at UN to MNE, September 30, 1981, AHPR, CC0210/3747.

[35] Francisco Pinto Balsemão, *Memórias*, 514–15.

[36] Maria de Lourdes Pintasilgo had been PM of the V Constitutional Government (1979–80). A Catholic, she had various contacts with international social and civic organizations. She had been ambassador to UNESCO before being called to discharge this duty.

the annual debate at the UNGA.[37] In pursuing this strategy, a new set of actions was implemented that represented an intensification of Portugal's diplomatic pressure. Contacts with FRETILIN in order to discuss a joint position were also incremented. However, the hesitations that characterized the position of Portugal up to that moment had left deep scars, and as time passed it became increasingly evident that the support of the international community to the cause of Timor-Leste was shallow.[38]

Futscher Pereira became MNE in June 1982. He insisted that "the tendency to erase the problem in the international arena is irreversible and independent of our efforts and enthusiasm one might develop to break or reverse it. . . . Nothing will lead Jakarta to reconsider its position and to recognize that the integration of Timor was not a genuine process of self-determination." And he added:

> [T]he conclusion is clear: if one wishes to serve Portuguese interests and to contribute to the amelioration of the fate of the Timorese people, the best is to adopt a new line of political action that allows us to put an end to the quarrel with Indonesia before the international community decides to throw this case into oblivion. . . . One must prevent the country to fall into an illusion and repeat previous mistakes. A high-level intervention seems imperious that accepts the inevitability of dialogue with Indonesia, with all its consequences. . . . On the other hand, this idea imposes an effort to prepare the public opinion and the political parties for such a painful as an inevitable outcome.[39]

Futscher Pereira's conclusion was extremely sensitive to internal public opinion. The risk existed that a possible rejection of the annual resolution proposal at the UNGA would be interpreted as a major victory for Indonesia. In such a context, Portugal hesitated as to the best course of action to be presented before the UNGA. After sending instructions to all embassies in view of amassing support for whatever Portugal would propose, in late October it became clear that defeat was in sight. In order to guarantee minimal room for maneuvering and safeguarding the interests of Portugal and Timor, it was then decided to cosponsor a resolution proposal that was submitted to the vote—after having been deeply discussed with FRETILIN and the countries that lent this movement support. Resolution 37/30 was approved by a mere four votes on November 23, 1982. It was a bitter victory. But it served the ultimate goals of the Portuguese strategy: the resolution conferred a mandate to the UNSG to initiate consultations with the parts with a view to explore solutions leading to a global settlement of the Timor-Leste issue. It was up to the UNSG to come up with a solution. In any case, the main goal of Portugal had been achieved: to discreetly negotiate with Indonesia an autonomy status for Timor, bearing in mind the status quo. Should Indonesia accept to talk in this context, it would be implicitly acknowledging that the Timor issue was not one located in the domestic but in the international arena.

---

[37] Both these plans were exposed in Pintasilgo's memos (February 15, 1982 and March 9, 1982), Centro de Documentação 25 de Abril—Universidade de Coimbra (CD25A), Maria de Lourdes Pintasilgo (MLP) archive, docs. 07813.040, 07813.041.

[38] FRETILIN criticized frequently Portugal's lack of involvement at the UN. José Ramos-Horta referred to the lack of support he received for his action in New York. José Ramos-Horta, *Amanhã em Díli* (Lisboa: D. Quixote, 1994), 215, 218.

[39] Memorandum, Futscher Pereira, September 22, 1982, AHPR, CC0210/3747.

For the Portuguese authorities, the period right after the approval of Resolution 37/30 was lived under the belief that the integration of Timor into Indonesia was irreversible. The constitutional revision of 1982 kept the reference to Timor's independence, but this was no more than an ideal without international support.[40] Pragmatism dictated that one had to find a solution harmonizing the international laws on the peoples' right to self-determination with the Portuguese own ones. It was paramount to circumvent the constitutional wording of "independence" and assume it as a metonymy for "self-determination." The real issue was thus: how could "self-determination" be guaranteed?

Both the presidency and the government considered various theoretical hypotheses: to stage some kind of an electoral act under international supervision, the eventual recognition of the annexation by the Timorese population, or the emergence of some special form of self-determination that might legitimize the integration by means of granting the territory with some kind of autonomy. Considering the practical difficulties involved in the first two hypotheses—one because Indonesia would not agree to it, the other because it would face the opposition of the Timorese population and of FRETILIN— the last was the one offering better prospects. However, the possibility of negotiating with a view to obtaining some form of autonomy—and not necessarily independence as Portugal was legally bound to support—required basic and controversial premises.

In the first half of 1983, several decisions were made on the course of action— and kept from public scrutiny. First, it was assumed that the strict wording of the constitution prevented a solution, and the issue should be handled as a question of self-determination and not purely independence. It was deemed necessary to establish direct conversations with Indonesia. The possibility to negotiate the deployment of a special UN mission to Timor-Leste under the auspices of the SG was also admitted. Finally, the proposal should be formulated for an autonomy status for the territory that would satisfy Indonesia, Portugal, and the international community as the materialization of the right to self-determination.[41]

A new government was installed on June 9, 1983. For the remainder of the year, no new step was made at the UN, but the conflict between PR and government was kept alive. The PR convened the newly installed Council of State on March 30, 1984, specifically to discuss the Timor issue. Above all, the PR wanted an agreement on a concrete working plan, defining the ultimate goals and the minimum acceptable goals for the negotiation with Indonesia under UN auspices. The meeting was not conclusive, mainly because there were diverging interpretations of the principles enshrined in section 297 of the Constitution. Some councilors stressed the need to be coherent, while others argued for pragmatism. Another point of contention was the role to be attributed to FRETILIN in the context of UN initiatives.[42]

---

[40] The constitutional revision of 1982 was made at a time when there were no conditions to modify its main principles. Constitutional law 1/82 (September 30) replaced section 307 with section 297, keeping its wording except in its number 2 where the reference to the extinguished Council of the Revolution was removed.

[41] A record of the approaches to this issue between 1983–84 appears in a letter from MNE Jaime Gama to PR, April 12, 1984, AHD/MNE, GPE Timor, pt. 3.

[42] Minutes, Council of State, March 30, 1984, AHPR-CE; Memorandum PR/CE/22 by Maria de Lourdes Pintasilgo, March 30, 1984, AHPR, CC0210/1866.

Delays in finding a way to move on, and the need to keep Timor-Leste in the UN agenda and not raise criticism for the slowness in initiating consultations, led to a compromise in New York by which the SG would present interim reports and postpone the final one. The Timor issue was also raised in Geneva at UN HRC. But Indonesia mobilized a strong lobby and in 1985 managed to approve a vote against the Portuguese positions.[43]

The way ahead implied conversation with Indonesia in the frame defined by the mandate conferred on the UNSG by Resolution 37/30. These would only start in 1984 and have six rounds (November 12–16, 1984; January 7–9, March 18–22; May 28–31, June 24–28; and August 19–22, 1985). On the table were proposals for the repatriation of former Portuguese civil servants and the return to Timor of a small group of refugees. Memos were exchanged regarding religious aspects (i.e., the protection of the Catholic Church), as well as the so-called "cultural legacy" of its population (mostly aspects referring to Portugal's marks and less to the ancestral traditions of the Timorese). Indonesia provided information on the current social and economic conditions in the territory. In practical terms, questions were avoided that pertained to the key differences between Portugal and Indonesia—the openly political issues: the illegitimacy of the annexation and the right to self-determination.

As the negotiating rounds drew to a close, President Eanes upgraded his criticism of the new government for lack of adequate lobbying that resulted in the loss at the HRC. Weak investment in publicly criticizing Indonesia was also brought up together with the alleged failure of the government to engage with NGOs at the national and international levels. These were very active, and the presidency sought to keep good relations with them. Exploring the contribution of the Catholic Church, both at the Vatican and those provided by Mgr. Ximenes Belo[44]—who was secretly in Lisboa in July 1985, where he met with PM Mário Soares and MNE Jaime Gama—was deemed insufficient. Articulation with FRETILIN, the actual leader of the internal Resistance, was regarded as undervalued. The activity of the national diplomats engaged in the New York talks was not well regarded given that Indonesia seemed to come out of them in a favorable position—a fact that was rendered clear by the uncritical acceptance of their reports conveying "positive" views on the situation in Timor. The president also noted that Portugal had not reacted to Indonesian president Suharto's and Australian PM Bob Hawke's statements of August 1985, both praising Indonesian sovereignty over Timor in disrespect with the negotiations being pursued in New York. Finally, there seemed to be no positive movement toward securing an autonomy status for Timor.[45]

---

[43] See Susana Vaz Patto, "Breve História da Política Portuguesa de Direitos Humanos," in *Portugal e os Direitos Humanos nas Nações Unidas*, ed. Ana Helena Marques, Carmen Silvestre, and Margarida Lages (Lisboa: Instituto Diplomático, 2017), 35–45; and Ana Gomes, "Direitos Humanos: o nosso soft e hard power. Por Timor-Leste e não só," in Marques, Silvestre, and Lages, *Portugal e os Direitos Humanos nas Nações Unidas*, 53–64.

[44] Carlos Filipe Ximenes Belo, Timorese priest, was appointed Apostolic Administrator of the Díli Diocese, after the resignation of bishop Martinho da Costa Lopes in 1983, and became the head of the Timor-Leste Catholic Church. He would be consecrated bishop in 1988.

[45] This sort of criticism is contained in various documents produced by the presidency and drawn by Pintasilgo's team, and then transferred to the correspondence between PR and PM. Among others, see PR memo July 22, 1985, CD25A, MLP, doc 07083.033; letter PR to PM, August 20, 1985, AHPR, CC0210/3746; summary of New York talks, August 22, 1985, AHPR, CC0210/3746; PM draft letter to PR on Suharto's statements, August 29, 1985, ADH/MNE, GPE Timor, pt. 18; letter PR to PM, September 5, 1985, AHPR,

Even though the president's criticism was well-grounded, there were at the time severe constraints in Portugal to the development of a more incisive diplomatic action. The government was in a caretaker position since late June, a new one being elected in October and sworn in in November. The president was about to leave office in March 1986. Mário Soares would win the presidential election and replace Eanes. The political conjuncture did not bode well for a rapid move in engaging Indonesia to discuss the critical aspects of the Timor issue.

1986–91: Looking for Alternative Paths to Return to the Principles

Contrary to the "treading water" attitude he had sustained as PM, Mário Soares as PR adopted a different attitude. If his government could be accused of not pursuing an incisive action and use soft terms not to antagonize Indonesia, Soares as PR would impose, right from the start, a substantial strategic shift, adopting a firm stance.[46]

One of his first decisions on this issue, conveyed to the new PM Cavaco Silva, consisted of refusing to accept the terms of a memorandum of understanding that the UN Undersecretary-General had tendered to the Portuguese diplomats in New York. This memorandum supported the deployment of an observation mission to accompany the Indonesian legislative elections of 1987, supposed to confirm the actual participation of the Timorese population in those polls, following what a report would be drawn paving the way for a new resolution to be presented to the UNGA stating that the self-determination issue had been solved. In other words: there would be no referendum nor was any question regarding self-determination supposed to be included in the ballot paper.[47]

Mário Soares would then press the government to take additional measures. A key factor to be used henceforth was the mobilization of European political cooperation, given that Portugal had acceded the European Economic Community on January 1, 1986, and was thus in a position to influence its partners to change their positions of not antagonizing Indonesia. He also pressed for the need to insist on the problem of the absence of Indonesian guarantees on human rights, leading to redefining the status of actions at the UN HRC in Geneva. In New York, Soares insisted that the issue of a popular consultation ought to be brought up in the conversations that could be considered as

---

CC0210/3747; memo PR to PM, September 16, 1985, AHPR, CC0210/3747; minutes of a meeting between PR and government on the issue of Timor, September 20, 1985, AHPR, CC0210/3746; comments by MNE to PR memo, October 17, 1985, AHPR, CC0210/3746.

[46] Mário Soares would claim, in an interview of 1997, that the "treading water" approach had been essential to allow the Timor issue to become visible in the eyes of the world public opinion, giving the Timorese Resistance enough time to assert itself internally and externally and allowing the Timorese Catholic Church—mainly through Bishop Ximenes Belo—to assume the representation of the very identity of its people. See Maria João Avillez, *Soares. O Presidente* (Lisboa: Círculo de Leitores, 1997), 234–35. A meeting between Soares and Monsignor Belo that took place at the Nuncio's residence in Lisboa in July 1985 is supposed to have been critical for the change of heart of the future president, as he realized through the information he received that the Indonesian repression was indeed intense, the people supported the guerrilla fighters, and there was a generalized sentiment among the population not to accept the annexation. See João Pedro Henriques, *Ana Gomes. A vida e o mundo* (Lisboa: Palimpsesto, 2020), 100–3.

[47] The text of the memorandum can be found as an appendix to Telegram 143, Mission at the UN to MNE, March 12, 1986, AHPR, CC0210/3747; Legal opinion issued by the presidency's advisory team, April 3, 1986, AHPR, CC0210/3752.

reasonable by Portugal as administering power, by the Timorese population, and by the international community. There could be no confusion with Indonesian elections. In this mood, he told PM Cavaco Silva that "in the time between his government and his election for the presidency things had moved quickly but in a dangerous way: there was no guarantee that Indonesian elections, performed by an authoritarian regime, would be free and not constitute a farce." Soares further suggested the government should study carefully the political evolution in Southeast Asia, where the Marcos regime in the Philippines had crumbled in 1986, possibly creating difficulties for the Indonesian regime, a reason why it would be necessary to "gain us some time." Raising the need for free elections in Timor could be a way to buy that precious time, waiting for the right moment for Indonesia to be forced to alter its stance. In the meantime, should Indonesia persist in creating obstacles, "it would be better to maintain the current situation, and in case Portugal was defeated at the UNGA, it could still claim to behave in a principled way and fight for its rights till they were fulfilled."[48]

In his memoirs published years later, PM Cavaco Silva has sought to dispel suspicions that he had opposed Soares's approach, claiming that the new president was following a different line from what he has sustained while leader of the government, espousing now a "tougher and harder line against Indonesia." He further claimed that there was "a perfect consonance" and coordination between PR and PM, including the overture to incorporate the Parliament in the discussion ring in order to avoid party divisions and the option to relaunch the issue in the international arena basing the national stance on the denunciation of human rights violations.[49] However, the change in attitude requested by Mário Soares was not entirely agreeable for the PM who believed in a "realistic" solution. Not long after Soares's inauguration, in a meeting with the new president that included the presence of the Foreign Minister Pedro Pires de Miranda, Cavaco Silva recalled that support for the Portuguese stance was losing ground at the UNGA, there was no qualitative changes requiring an alteration of the established policy, and said he understood the question as "a choice between interrupting the whole process until new evidence on the regional situation was amassed together with insights into what the members of EEC were willing to contemplate, or ascertain the extent to which the lines drawn by the Portuguese negotiators at the UN were prone to correction."[50] Above all, any change of orientation would be consequential for the Portuguese diplomacy and the foreign policy of the government given that different priorities would lead to an impasse in the ongoing conversations in New York that were on the verge of reaching an agreement allowing Portugal to "save its face," based on the UN acceptance of an eventual report to be produced by a commission appointed by the UNSG to observe the Timorese participation in the 1987 Indonesian elections.[51]

At the presidency, however, there was no inclination to go soft of principles. In a new meeting with the PM (May 1986), Mário Soares insisted he could not accept the replacement of an act of self-determination by the staging of Indonesian elections: "It is necessary to ascertain that, in the absence of a legitimate alternative to the exercise of the

---

[48] Minutes, meeting of PR with PM and MNE, April 4, 1986, AHPR/PR/CC/CC0210/3747.

[49] Aníbal Cavaco Silva, *Autobiografia Política* (Lisboa: Temas e Debates, 2002), 309–10.

[50] Minutes, meeting of PR with PM and MNE, April 4, 1985, AHPR/PR/CC/CC0210/3747.

[51] The impasse deriving from a return to the issue of self-determination as the key point would be commented on in his *Autobiografia Política*, 309–10.

right to self-determination, Portugal prefers things to remain as they are, pursuing efforts to re-establish a lawful situation and persisting in working loyally with the UNSG."[52] In the meeting of the State Council convened by Soares on July 29, the PM would still argue that the concept of self-determination was broad and encompassed different outcomes and that Portugal had never considered a referendum as a sine qua non condition for the case of Timor. The UNSG was about to end his term in office and there was no guarantee as to his reelection, fearing that this might entail the collapse of the terms of Resolution 37/30. For the PM, the Timor issue could only pursue its career at the UN if the UNGA took an initiative, and the deployment of an observation mission might provide grounds to postpone the debate and prevent its demise. The president, for his part, insisted on his previous stance, which represented a step back from accepting the fait accompli and a significant change in the policies that had been pursued by successive governments in the consultations with Indonesia. In a way, he was imposing a return to the 1974–75 sense of the Portuguese obligations toward Timor-Leste: dogmatic principles were better than pragmatic rationalism.

The reconsideration of the Portuguese strategy was consequential upon the tripartite conversations in New York. In April 1986, talks had resumed between Portugal, Indonesia, and a representative of the UNSG, and the basic document on the table requested the deployment of an observation mission to the Indonesian elections of 1987. Given the instructions issued by the PR, Portugal could not accept any initiative that might entail the legitimation of Indonesia's position. In order to overtake the impasse, the idea emerged to organize a visit to Timor-Leste by a number of Portuguese public figures with the backing of the national authorities.[53] In January 1987, the Portuguese government accepted that such an initiative could go ahead as a visit of members of the Parliament. This subsequently resulted in an invitation issued by the Speaker of the Indonesian Parliament to his Portuguese counterparts (January 23, 1988). Preparations for this visit would occupy most of the talks' agenda for the next few years.

The alleged consonance between PR and PM concealed a real divergence as to the acceptable solutions for Timor. To keep a strict defense of legal and moral principles implied the situation would drag on and confront an international community who favored good economic and political relations with Indonesia and would not respond to the pressing, humanitarian needs of the Timorese population and their human rights. To convince Indonesia to accept a popular consultation on the future of the territory did not seem realistic given that Jakarta persisted in defending its position with the very same old arguments. For the Portuguese government, a "realistic" solution had to be found elsewhere.

A modification in the government's position—albeit not officially assumed— would emerge when the new executive derived from the July 1987 elections presented its program to the Parliament. Cavaco Silva obtained an absolute majority and his government program contained a subtle change of orientation that was noted by the presidency staff. It did not mention the principle of self-determination and independence

---

[52] Memorandum, PR, May 21, 1986, AHPR, CC/0210/3747.

[53] This topic is further developed in Zélia Pereira and Rui Graça Feijó, "Crónica de uma Missão Falhada: o atribulado projeto de visita de uma delegação parlamentar portuguesa a Timor-Leste," *Proceedings of the TLSA International Symposium on Santa Cruz Massacre: 30 Years On* (forthcoming).

of Timor-Leste, even though it referred to the ongoing talks in New York. Speaking before the Parliament, PM used a "substitutive formula" and expressed the need to find a "dignified solution" safeguarding "the religious and cultural identity of the People of Timor-Leste" and the "Portuguese cultural presence," all within a realistic framework guaranteeing "the dignity of Portugal." At the presidency, Cavaco Silva's speech was interpreted as "a shift of position, whose critical point is the abandonment by the government of the request of an act of self-determination as a necessary condition for settling the Timor issue."[54]

The Portuguese oscillation between principles and harsh reality and the consequence that might be derived from the projected parliamentarians' visit to the territory were both reflected in the upcoming constitutional revision in 1989. The new section 293 (updating previous section 307 [1976] and 297 [1982]) kept point 2 unchanged. However, its title ("Self-Determination and Independence for Timor-Leste") and point 1 ("Portugal remains bound to its responsibilities, in the light of international law, to promote and guarantee the right of Timor-Leste to self-determination and independence") represented a formal opening to new political solutions not necessarily through independence. Hitherto, independence was the only constitutionally permitted solution; henceforth, self-determination without independence was now a parallel possibility. One might think that this was only one word that was added. But the room for maneuver for considering new mechanisms to regulate the recognition of Timor's integration—perhaps as soon as the parliamentarians' visit took place—was now established.

Among the Portuguese political authorities, the parliamentarians' visit was not consensual. In March 1988, PR convened a meeting of the Council of State specifically dedicated to that issue. The generalized opinion was that Portugal should exercise prudence.[55] A major concern was that the mission would be composed of several members of an organ of sovereignty. Even though in constitutional terms the Parliament was devoid of responsibilities regarding the situation in Timor-Leste, the visit could well be interpreted by Indonesia and several important countries as an official Portuguese delegation with a strong political sense. Moreover, it ran the risk of meaning the abandonment by Portugal of the requirement to hold a genuine act of self-determination. In the Parliament itself, several quarters harbored doubts on the wisdom of the visit, and thus the answer to the Indonesian invitation was conditional on several points.[56]

Conversations with Indonesia in New York on the terms of reference for the visit were not easy. Indonesia raised a plethora of difficulties in response to the conditions set by Portugal. Between the first suggestion that the visit might take place (1987) and the agreement on its final terms of reference (1991), more than four years elapsed. During those years, the Portuguese authorities struggled to find common ground among themselves, a situation that was extended to the various branches of the Timorese Resistance, both inside and outside Timor-Leste, and even to key actors such as the Catholic Church. The political impact of the visit and the consequences that might arise from public demonstrations

---

[54] Advice, PR staff, September 15, 1987, AHPR/PR/CC/CC0210/3752.

[55] Minutes, Council of State meeting, March 9, 1988, AHPR-CE.

[56] Among those who harbored reservations one must count Jorge Sampaio, then parliamentary leader of the Socialist Party, who would be president from 1996. See Memorandum, PR staff, on a meeting with Sampaio, June 18, 1988, AHPR, CC0210/2478. See also the response given by the Speaker of the House to the letter from his Indonesian counterpart, July 19, 1988, Arquivo Histórico Parlamentar (AHP), COM 679/4.

inside Timor-Leste—both by the resisting population and by the Indonesian forces—were subject to competing interpretations. Echoes of preparations being made in Timor-Leste to welcome the parliamentarians' delegation reached Lisboa, sparking fears they might get out of control. Also, the obstacles the Indonesian negotiators were raising against the freedom of movement of the parliamentarians and the composition of the full delegation—which included unfriendly journalists to the Indonesian cause—weighed on the evaluation of the benefits of the visit. Altogether, they were thought to be sufficiently important to justify the postponement of the visit that was planned for early November 1991. What happened in the immediate aftermath is well known. On November 12, the Indonesian military opened fire on a peaceful demonstration heading toward Santa Cruz cemetery in central Dili, killing hundreds. Footage of the massacre recorded by Max Stahl—an eyewitness together with other journalists like Amy Goodman and Alan Nairn—was broadcast worldwide. The struggle of Timor-Leste for self-determination and respect for human rights could no longer be ignored by international public opinion.

Indonesian diplomat and foreign minister Ali Alatas refers in his memoirs on the Timor issue that in the course of the New York talks to find a "comprehensive, just and internationally acceptable" solution for the problem, Indonesia had accepted all compromise plans submitted by the UN side. First, the deployment of an international observation mission to the 1987 elections. Later, the invitation to a Portuguese parliamentary delegation. On both occasions, Portugal had agreed in principle to those terms only to withdraw "at the last minute."[57] Alatas is right, but for Portugal those changes of position meant that it was not possible to dilute moral and legal principles in political pragmatism.

It was increasingly clear that the Timorese population would not easily bow before a solution representing the recognition of an integration they did not desire, as the events surrounding the Santa Cruz massacre had made plainly visible. Still, a long way to reconcile the harsh reality of facts with the moral principles needed to be traveled. For Portugal, the way forward consisted in keeping the flame alive at the UN until international pressure and Indonesian domestic problems would combine to change the terms of reference for the desired solution. This would only happen in 1999, after the fall of Suharto, when the new president B. J. Habibie announced he would support the staging of a referendum in Timor-Leste. The terms for the referendum were negotiated again in New York, resulting in the May 5 agreement. On August 30, 1999, a UN-sponsored and supervised referendum was finally organized. An overwhelming 78.5 percent of the Timorese rejected the option for an enlarged autonomy within the Republic of Indonesia and instead chose independence.

Conclusion

In the international arena, the "Timor-Leste issue" after 1976 was mostly circumscribed to the realm of human rights violations, in parallel with a tacit acceptance of its annexation by Indonesia. This was visible in the dwindling support for the UNGA resolutions relating to this question. The key issue of assuring the exercise of the right to self-determination was second to the humanitarian one.

---

[57] Ali Alatas, *The Pebble in the Shoe. The Diplomatic Struggle for East Timor* (Jacarta: Aksara Karunia, 2006), vxii.

The Portuguese Constitution, both in its 1976 wording and in the new version of 1982, stood as a rigid factor conditioning the development of a policy addressing the Timor issue, slightly eased in the 1989 revision. First, it imposed a joint supervision shared between the PR and the government, excluding the Parliament from direct involvement. Second, it stipulated that independence was the goal to achieve. More than defending those principles guiding the Portuguese decolonization in Africa and the ones sustained by the UN in the field of self-determination rights, the constitutional provisions rigidified the acceptable solutions, mainly when competing responsibilities of PR and PM came into play. It was actually difficult to find a solid consensus among leading politicians in regard to the Timor question. Independence, though it was a constitutional mandate, was soon assumed to be an unattainable ideal—but it was not so easy to walk away from moral and legal principles that sustained self-determination. Other possible solutions were conceived as ways of sidestepping the rigid constitutional mandate. Between 1976 and 1986, the great fluctuation of governments (there were ten in Portugal whereas in Indonesia only two foreign ministers were active) and frictions with the PR were mirrored in ambiguous stances and the weakness of the national diplomacy. However, the same legal rigidity and the unwillingness to abandon moral principles may have imposed delays in finding a solution accepting the integration of Timor into Indonesia, but these, in turn, permitted that at the end of the day those principles won over pragmatism, avoiding a premature end to the dispute and creating the necessary conditions for a new international conjuncture to emerge and favor the Timor cause—a move that became clear under Mário Soares as PR.

Mário Soares's change of mind opened the way for a more solid course of action, grounded on a wider national consensus, even though competition between political realism and principled stances was kept very much alive. Accepting to send a parliamentary delegation to Timor after pondering the serious challenge it posed, contributed to gaining time and avoiding a rupture at the New York talks. Events surrounding the Santa Cruz massacre, in the wake of the cancellation of that visit, vindicated Mário Soares's stance. These conveyed a clear sign: the resistance inside Timor was real and the desire for an autonomous future was strong. Portugal could not accept any solution resulting in the recognition of the Indonesian annexation as a fait accompli. Conversely, the strategy ought to be redrafted and wait for political change in Jakarta, as Soares had expressed in 1986 when he turned down the terms of the proposed agreement. After all, the passing of time—a weapon Indonesia thought would play in its favor, confident as it was of the erosion of the Timor issue in the international arena and the acceptance of its annexation—turned the table and allowed Timor-Leste to remain as an open issue at the UN, to conquer a great deal of visibility after the broadcasting of Santa Cruz massacre footage in 1991 and to successfully accede independence after a genuine act of self-determination in 1999.

Human Rights in Timor-Leste's Struggle for Independence

Amy Rothschild

Introduction

This article investigates the role of human rights—specifically the role of human rights discourses and practices—in Timor-Leste's struggle for independence from Indonesia from 1975 to 1999.[1] It examines the context within which Timor's Resistance movement increasingly began to employ human rights beginning in the 1980s. It also examines how human rights were used by Timor's Resistance movement and the effects of this employment of human rights on the movement. I use the Timor case to make larger arguments about the nature of human rights and human rights activism and about the relationships between human rights, anticolonialism, and the right to self-determination.

I argue that Timor's Resistance movement began to increasingly employ human rights in the 1980s with the primary aim of appealing to the international community—specifically, the major Western powers.[2] The central way that Timorese employed human rights discourses and practices was to present themselves to the international community as innocent, suffering victims of human rights violations whom the international

Amy Rothschild (PhD, JD) is Assistant Professor, sociolegal studies, Ithaca College. The author would like to thank the anonymous reviewer of this article, as well as Dr. Nancy Postero, for their extremely helpful comments.

[1] I define "human rights" as a transnational normative system, characterized by its self-declared universalistic nature and linked to the United Nations and the 1948 Universal Declaration of Human Rights. Unless otherwise stated, throughout the article I use "human rights" as a shorthand for "human rights discourses and practices."

[2] These key states included the United States, Canada, Britain, and Australia. Throughout the article I use "international community" as a shorthand for "major Western powers."

community had a moral responsibility to protect. This political, strategic use of human rights was pivotal to Timor's ultimate achievement of independence.[3]

I make the following claims based on the Timor case. First, the Timor case shows us that human rights can be successfully employed as a tool to contest existing power relations. Put differently, the Timor case illustrates the political nature—and the emancipatory potential—of human rights. Second, the Timor case shows us that at least in some contexts, human rights work to achieve substantive political change, including, in this case, a winning of self-determination and state sovereignty, due to perceptions of their apoliticality and the apoliticality of their categories, including the category of the innocent victim. The Timor case also points to a problematic outcome of these perceptions of apoliticality: the images of suffering Timorese victims consumed by Western audiences via media have had the effect of obscuring the agency of the Timorese who worked to produce such images and give them meaning. Finally, I argue that the pivotal role played by human rights in Timor's struggle for independence serves to challenge claims of a strict binary between anticolonialism and human rights, or between the right to self-determination and the rest of the human rights corpus.

This article engages with other literature on the use of human rights in Timor Leste's struggle for independence from Indonesia. More specifically it adds to a small but emerging body of literature that focuses on the use of human rights discourses by Timor's internal Resistance movement, as opposed to by Timor's Catholic Church, by the international solidarity movement that supported Timor, or by the Resistance's external diplomatic front.[4] The article also engages with scholarship on the politics of human rights and human activism, including in the Cold War era; this includes scholarship that examines the relationship between anticolonialism, the right to self-determination, and human rights. Finally, the article contributes to mainstream histories of human rights movements. Despite the central role that human rights played in Timor's achievement of independence, Timor-Leste is largely left out of these histories, which tend to focus on human rights movements in Latin America and eastern Europe.[5]

The article proceeds as follows: I begin by examining the early days of Timor's Resistance movement, from the mid- to late 1970s, when it was primarily guided by a politics of anticolonialism. Then, I turn to the Resistance's embrace of human rights discourses in the early 1980s. After discussing the Resistance's motivations for this embrace, I discuss how human rights discourses and practices were employed by Timor's Resistance movement and to what effect. Finally, I turn to the larger implications of the Timor case. I examine what the Timor case tells us more generally about human rights and about the relationships between human rights, politics, agency, and anticolonialism. I conclude with a summation of the article's main points. The article relies on data from

---

[3] The Frente Revolucionária de Timor-Leste Independente (Fretilin) had proclaimed the independence of the Democratic Republic of East Timor on November 18, 1975, less than two weeks before the Indonesian invasion. Timorese voted for independence in a referendum on August 30, 1999; it gained official independence on May 20, 2002.

[4] By the 1980s, Timor's Resistance movement was divided into "three fronts": the armed, clandestine, and diplomatic fronts. The first two can be considered the internal fronts.

[5] Geoffrey Robinson, "Human Rights History from the Ground Up: The Case of East Timor," in *The Human Rights Paradox: Universality and Its Discontents*, ed. Steve J. Stern and Scott Straus (Madison: University of Wisconsin Press), 55. See also Marisa Ramos-Goncalves, "Genealogies of Human Rights Ideas in Timor-Leste: 'Kultura', Modernity, and Resistance," *Nómadas* no. 53 (2021): 53, https://doi.org/10.30578/nomadas.n53a3.

ongoing work and ethnographic fieldwork in Timor-Leste beginning in 2002, as well as secondary sources.[6]

Timor's Early Resistance Movement: An "Anti-Ideology"

The earliest incarnation of Timor's Resistance movement, the political party Associação Social-Democratica Timorense (ASDT), came into existence on May 20, 1974, in the context of decolonization from Portugal, before the Indonesian invasion of Timor on December 7, 1975. Led by Timor's small, educated, urban elite, ASDT modeled itself on other third-world anticolonial nationalist liberation movements, particularly those in Portugal's African colonies.[7] ASDT's original platform of anticolonialism, anti-neocolonialism, anti-imperialism, and antidiscrimination, could in many ways be defined as an "anti-ideology."[8] At this time, the modern international or global human rights regime—established in 1948 with the adoption of the Universal Declaration of Human Rights (UDHR)—had existed for over two decades. Yet international human rights ideas, discourses, and practices played little role in the Resistance at this stage. In early 1975, ASDT, now renamed Frente Revolucionária de Timor-Leste Independente (Fretilin), did refer to the UDHR. Yet, as far as I have found, it was only in relation to the right to independence.[9]

Timor's Resistance movement continued to embrace anticolonial ideology, and maintain its distance from the human rights regime and its discourses, during the early years of the occupation, when civilians lived in the mountains with Forças Armadas da Libertação Nacional de Timor-Leste or Falintil in "liberated zones" outside of Indonesian control.[10] Fretilin took a more "radical" or "leftist" turn during this period, with Marxism declared Fretilin's official ideology in 1977.[11] In line with a Marxist critique of rights as "bourgeois hypocrisies,"[12] the social programs that the Resistance implemented at this time (programs that had been developed before the invasion) primarily focused on collective and economic emancipation, rather than on the individual and political freedoms associated with human rights.

During this period in the mountains, the Resistance maintained its distance not only from discourses of human rights, but from the international community at-large. As with

---

[6] I conducted ethnographic research for my anthropology PhD dissertation on the politics of memory of the Indonesian occupation in the summers of 2008 and 2009 and from 2011 to 2012 (I conducted follow-up research in 2022). I also spent a year in Timor from 2002 to 2003, when I interned at the Comissão de Acolhimento, Verdade e Reconciliação de Timor Leste (CAVR). I spent additional time living and volunteering in Timor in 2007.

[7] Jill Joliffe, *East Timor: Nationalism and Colonialism* (St. Lucia: University of Queensland Press, 1978), 63.

[8] Jan Eckel, "Human Rights and Decolonization: New Perspectives and Open Questions," *Humanity Journal* 1, no. 11 (2010): 115.

[9] See Joliffe, *East Timor*, 94. Fretilin officially declared Timor's independence on November 28, 1975, less than two weeks before the Indonesian invasion.

[10] Falintil was established on August 20, 1975.

[11] The Timor-Leste Commission for Reception, Truth and Reconciliation (CAVR), *Chega! The Final Report of the Timor-Leste Commission for Reception, Truth and Reconciliation (CAVR)*, KPG in cooperation with STP-CAVR, Jakarta, 2013, 5:16.

[12] Karl Marx, "On the Jewish Question," in *The Marx-Engels Reader*, ed. Robert C. Tucker, 2nd revised and enlarged ed. (New York: W. W. Norton & Company, 1978).

other anticolonial movements, Timor's Resistance movement emphasized the idea of "self-reliance"; many within the movement argued that the Resistance should refuse all foreign aid.[13] The main form of resistance to Indonesian rule from the time of the invasion through this period in the mountains was armed resistance, as led by Falintil. Armed resistance was viewed by leading anticolonial theorists at the time as coterminous with anticolonial ideology; it was deemed the "only possible path to liberation."[14] Significantly—and as will be discussed further below—violent resistance is seen to be at odds with a politics centered around the use of human rights, particularly in the post-Cold War era.

Motivation for the Turn Toward Human Rights: Appealing to the West

It was only in the early 1980s, after the surrender of Timor's civilian population from the mountains that Timor's regrouped Resistance movement began to deemphasize anticolonial discourses and practices and embrace human rights discourses and practices. What accounted for this shift? A main factor was the realization that independence would not come about through a military victory and would only be gained with international support[15]—specifically, with support from the major Western powers.[16] Despite the fact that in 1975 and 1976 the United Nations Security Council had recognized Indonesia's violation of Timor's right to self- determination with its invasion,[17] there was growing agreement within Timor's Resistance movement that the use of anticolonial rhetoric was not the best way to gain Western support. One reason was the late timing of Timor's struggle for independence—there was a sense by many that mainstream decolonization had already run its course. A second reason was the West's growing international disillusionment with the idea of anticolonialism (and the corresponding right to self-determination).[18] The historian Samuel Moyn has argued that this disillusionment was a result of the reality that some former colonies had become authoritarian, violent, and antidemocratic—in other words, not supportive of human rights.[19]

[13] A principle of self-reliance was officially adopted by the Resistance in 1977. CAVR, *Chega*, 3:77.

[14] Frantz Fanon, *The Wretched of the Earth*, trans Richard Philcox, preface John-Paul Sartre, foreword by Homi K. Bhabha, reprint ed. (New York: Grove Press, 2005), 61.

[15] CAVR, *Chega*, 5:40.

[16] Many non-Western nations had already offered their support to Timor: the newly independent African nations of Angola, Cape Verde, Guinea-Bissau, Mozambique, and San Tomé and Príncipe had all recognized Timor-Leste's independence when it was declared in 1975; China and Vietnam had "extended their warm congratulations." CAVR, *Chega*, 5:58.

[17] The United Nations Declaration of the Granting of Independence to Colonial Countries and Peoples (the Declaration on Decolonization) was passed in 1960; the right to self-determination was also included in Articles 1 of the International Covenant on Civil and Political Rights, and the International Covenant on Economic, Social and Cultural Rights, both ratified in 1966. On December 22, 1975 and April 22, 1976, the United Nations Security Council passed resolutions calling on Indonesia to withdraw troops from Timor and for Portugal to cooperate with the United Nations to enable East Timorese people to freely exercise the right to self-determination. While 1976 was the last time until 1999 that the Security Council considered the issue, from 1975 to 1982, there was an annual affirmation in the General Assembly calling on Indonesia to withdraw from Timor and affirming Timor's right to self-determination. Geoffrey Robinson, If You Leave Us Here, We Will Die: How Genocide Was Stopped in East Timor (Princeton: Princeton University Press, 2010), 79. See also Robinson, "Human Rights History from the Ground Up," 40.

[18] Bradley Simpson, "Denying the 'First Right': The United States, Indonesia, and the Ranking of Human Rights by the Carter Administration, 1976–1980," *The International History Review* 31, no. 4 (2009).

[19] Samuel Moyn, *The Last Utopia: Human Rights in History*, reprint ed. (Cambridge, MA: Belknap Press, 2012), 118.

If an anticolonial framework wasn't helpful or was even counterproductive in winning the support of the West, human rights provided a promising new framework for several reasons. First, of course, was the reality that since the invasion the Indonesian regime had been committing the most egregious abuses of basic human rights in Timor, including the right to life. Second, by the 1980s the global human rights regime had become increasingly prominent. This prominence increased further after the end of the Cold War, when human rights "became an explicit foreign policy objective of an increasing number of Western states."[20] With the end of the Cold War, there was now an increased ability to criticize Indonesia in human rights terms; the Indonesian occupation could no longer be linked to Jakarta's role as a "bastion of anti-Communism in Southeast Asia."[21] Also relevant, a new norm of "humanitarian intervention" emerged in the 1990s, justified in relation to human rights. Finally, in embracing human rights practices and discourses, Timor's Resistance was able to work together with a growing international solidarity movement that supported Timor, a movement that itself primarily relied on human rights discourses and practices in its advocacy efforts.

If the primary reason that Timor's Resistance movement increasingly embraced human rights discourses and practices was to appeal to the major Western powers more successfully, a secondary reason—albeit one that is related, as international support hinged on presenting a unified internal front—was to widen support for Timor's Resistance movement within Timor. The Resistance's use of a human rights framework helped it to gain the support of both Timor's Church and Timor's *gerasaun foun* (new generation). Both entities had had conflicts with the anticolonial ideology of Fretilin.

Human Rights as Catastrophe Prevention: Timorese and Innocent, Suffering Victimhood

The legal scholar Henry Steiner has argued that the global human rights movement has two interrelated but distinct missions that are often confused: human rights as utopian politics and human rights as catastrophe prevention. In line with this characterization, I suggest there were two main ways that Timor's Resistance employed human rights in its struggle. First, the Resistance embraced the utopian mission of the human rights movement, using human rights discourses in its assertions of what the Resistance was struggling for and what an independent future Timorese state would stand for. The Resistance no longer wanted to achieve a revolution aimed at the "total abolition of colonialism"[22]; nor did it simply want to achieve national liberation. Rather, the Resistance now wanted to form an independent state founded on human rights principles. As José Alexandre Gusmão ("Xanana") stated in 1987: Timor's Resistance was "committed to building a free and democratic nation, based on respect for the freedoms of thought, association and expression, as well as complete respect of Universal Human Rights."[23]

---

[20] Robinson, "Human Rights History from the Ground Up," 42.

[21] Bradley Simpson, "'Illegally and Beautifully': The United States, the Indonesian Invasion of East Timor and the International Community, 1974–76," *Cold War History* 5, no. 3 (2005): 282. See also David Webster, "Non-state Diplomacy: East Timor 1975–1999," *Portuguese Studies Review* 1, no. 1 (2003): 19

[22] Quoted in Joliffe, *East Timor*, 74.

[23] Quoted in CAVR, *Chega*, 7.1:88. Of course, human rights as future-oriented utopian politics and human rights as catastrophe prevention are connected: in declaring an intention to construct a future state based on human rights principles, the Resistance also implied the future state would be free of catastrophe.

Second, and more significantly, the Resistance appealed to the catastrophe prevention goal or dimension of the human rights movement, aimed at "stopping the massive disasters that have plagued humanity."[24] It did this by using human rights discourses and practices to call attention to the violence being committed against Timorese by the Indonesian regime—and to the resulting Timorese suffering and victimhood. With this use of human rights, the Resistance's argument to the major Western powers for self-determination essentially shifted from self-determination being a right or end in and of itself—a right that was violated with Indonesia's illegal invasion in 1975—to independence or self-determination being a means to the greater end of securing basic individual human rights. The Resistance and its supporters made this argument both implicitly and explicitly at different times.[25] An instance of this argument being made explicit occurred in 1993 when Resistance spokesperson Abe Barreto Soares testified to the United Nations Commission on Human Rights that "there will be more human rights abuses in East Timor as long as there is no peaceful solution for the East Timor problem."[26]

Timorese employed several tools in the human rights "repetoire"[27] to call attention to Timorese suffering and victimhood. One key tool or human rights practice was the documentation of violence. In the early years of the occupation, this typically took the form of making lists or reports; as early as 1983, Gusmão ordered Fretilin officials to start making lists of civilians who had been killed, disappeared, tortured, and detained.[28] Documentation was then smuggled to supporters outside of Timor (funneling information out of Timor was one of the main tasks of the Resistance's clandestine front). When possible, particularly after 1989 when Timor was slightly more opened to international visitors, Timorese arranged for foreigners inside of Timor to witness and document human rights violations themselves. In addition, Timorese were sometimes able to conduct their own visual documentation of violations with smuggled-in cameras or video cameras.

Another key tool or practice involved employing the language and vocabulary of human rights.[29] Resistance leaders made statements—included in various documents such as peace plans, press releases, and letters—denouncing the human rights violations

---

[24] Henry Steiner, Session on "International Human Rights Perspectives and Notions of Liberalism" (Conference on Religion and State: An Interdisciplinary Roundtable Discussion, part of the Harvard Law School Human Rights Program, Vouliagmeni, Greece, October 1999), 52. The catastrophe prevention view of human rights is largely synonymous with a "minimalist" view of human rights.

[25] The first prominent public call for a referendum on self-rule had been made years earlier, in 1989, by Bishop Belo (the head of the Catholic Church in Timor). Belo had similarly linked the need for Timorese self-determination to the ongoing violence of the Indonesian regime. Specifically, he had prefaced his assertion that "the people of Timor must be allowed to express their views on their future through a plebiscite" with a statement that Timorese "continue to die as a people and a nation." Belo made these assertations in a letter to the President of Portugal, the Pope, and the United Nations Secretary-General. Quoted in Catherine Scott, *East Timor: The Continuing Betrayal* (London: Catholic Institute for International Relations, 1996), 17.

[26] Abe Barreto Soares, "Timorese Statements at UNHRC," 1993, accessed May 3, 2015, https://groups.google .com/forum/#!topic/misc.activism.progressive/45j887qaTrY.

[27] Margaret Hagan, "The Human Rights Repertoire: Its Strategic Logic, Expectations and Tactics," *The International Journal of Human Rights* 14, no. 4 (2010).

[28] Robinson, "Human Rights History from the Ground Up," 40.

[29] Human rights language was often learned through links with foreign NGOs. These links were made most easily by Timorese activists studying in Indonesia, who connected to Indonesian human rights NGOs and activists through Indonesia's pro-democracy movement. See Robinson, "Human Rights History from the Ground Up," 43–44.

committed by the Indonesian regime and/or appealing for protection of Timorese human rights. These statements, which were directed at key international figures (including the Secretary-General of the United Nations), included references to general terms such as "human rights" and to documents or proclamations such as the "Universal Declaration of Human Rights." References were also made to specific human rights violations, such as "extrajudicial execution," "disappearance," "prisoner of conscience," and "genocide."[30] Along these lines, students often chanted or otherwise called for "human rights" at the nonviolent demonstrations that occurred in Timor after 1989.

Nonviolence, Timor's "Trauma Drama," and the Success of the Human Rights Strategy

I argue that the most significant human rights practice employed by Timor's Resistance movement to call attention to Timorese suffering and victimhood was the increased use of nonviolent forms of resistance. While in international law there is agreement that people can use violent resistance if their self-determination is being denied, in practice the victim-perpetrator binary that underlies human rights categorizes people as one or the other. The victim-perpetrator binary arguably became more pronounced after the Cold War, when, as multiple scholars have argued, the global human rights regime not only grew more prominent, but assumed a new form. Specifically, some scholars argue that in the post-Cold War era human rights merged with humanitarianism, increasingly emphasizing concern for the suffering of "powerless, helpless" victims.[31] Genocide prevention took on greater importance and a new norm of humanitarian intervention emerged.[32] An increased use of nonviolent methods of resistance by those trying to prove their victimhood—and a corresponding decreased use of methods deemed violence—thus became even more critical in this period.[33]

A "trauma drama" is a tragedy of suffering aimed at appealing to a transnational audience's sense of pity and sympathy.[34] It could be argued that Timorese had been engaged in the production of such a drama since the early 1980s, with their documentation efforts and their employment of the language and vocabulary of human rights. The metaphor becomes even more apt with the increased Timorese employment of nonviolent resistance. There were two pivotal "scenes," if you will, in Timor's trauma drama, both of which were critical to Timor gaining its independence. Notably, both hinged on the absence of Timorese violence in the face of Indonesian violence, thus presenting the Timorese people as ideal victims.

---

[30] Robinson, "Human Rights History from the Ground Up," 44. See Xanana Gusmao, *To Resist Is to Win!: The Autobiography of Xanana Gusmao with Selected Letters & Speeches* (Richmond, AUS: Aurora Books, 2000), 154, 156. See also Conselho Nacional de Resistencia Maubere, *CNRM Press Release*, 1993, accessed April 29, 2015, http://www.library.ohiou.edu/indopubs/1993/12/22/0000.html.

[31] Makau W. Mutua, "Savages, Victims, and Saviors: The Metaphor of Human Rights," *Harvard International Law Journal* 42, no. 1 (Winter 2001): 203.

[32] Moyn, *The Last Utopia*, 219. Referencing Henry Steiner, one could say after that in the post-Cold War era human rights increasingly embraced its anti-catastrophe mission.

[33] While Falintil's armed resistance became less central to the Resistance movement, Falintil continued to exist as a central Resistance institution throughout the occupation.

[34] Laleh Khalili, *Heroes and Martyrs of Palestine: The Politics of National Commemoration* (Cambridge: Cambridge University Press, 2007), 33–34

The first scene was the Santa Cruz massacre of November 12, 1991. Video footage of this massacre—which included shots of Indonesian troops firing on unarmed Timorese protesters, including women and children—was smuggled out of Timor and broadcast on televisions around the world within days. The massacre momentarily turned Timor into a front-page story, resulting in widespread international condemnation of Indonesia's human rights record in Timor and the "initiation of some of the first concrete measures" designed to discipline Indonesia.[35] Historians agree that the massacre—which also resulted in the exponential growth of the international solidarity movement in support of Timor—was a "watershed" moment in Timor's struggle for independence.[36]

The second pivotal scene resulted from the Resistance's decision to abstain from using armed violence, even in the form of the defense of the population-at-large, during the "scorched-earth campaign" conducted by the Indonesian military and militias in the period between the August 30, 1999 referendum and the arrival of international troops into Timor on September 20, 1999. Despite the large amount of Indonesian-led militia violence that had been committed in the months preceding the referendum, as well as threats by the Indonesian military and militias to "turn Timor to dust" should the population vote for independence, by August 12, under orders from Gusmão, Falintil had put all its troops in cantons to prove that it was not the source of the violence. After the referendum, the Indonesian military and the militias commenced killing at least 900 Timorese, transferring a quarter of Timor's population by force, mostly to Indonesian West Timor, and destroying 70 percent of Timor's infrastructure. When then-Commander-in-Chief of Falintil José Maria Vasconcelos ("Taur Matan Ruak" or "TMR") threatened to retaliate on September 7, Gusmão, speaking to Ruak by satellite phone, forbade this retaliation, no matter what the cost in human life and suffering. Gusmão did not want to risk forfeiting the international intervention that was the only hope for salvation.[37]

As with the Santa Cruz massacre, images of the post-referendum violence dominated the international news and led to massive worldwide protests calling for intervention.[38] These protests (and media campaigns) eventually caused the United States and other governments to agree to the idea of an armed international intervention to stop the violence. Historians have argued that without the post-referendum violence, international opinion would not have been sufficiently mobilized to make such an intervention possible.[39] However, critically, it wasn't the violence alone—or even the press images of the violence—that resulted in the intervention that secured Timorese independence. Rather, as David Webster has pointed out, it was the way that this violence fit into the already existing narrative of the situation in Timor, which posed a violent

---

[35] This included two statements from the United Nations Commission on Human Rights, issued in 1992 and 1993.

[36] While most observers have stressed the international effects of the massacre, others have noted the pivotal role the massacre played inside of Timor. See Dan Nicholson, "The Lorikeet Warriors: East Timorese New Generation Nationalist Resistance, 1989–1999." (Thesis, University of Melbourne, 2002), 23.

[37] CAVR, *Chega*, 3:146–47.

[38] Nicholas J. Wheeler and Tim Dunne, "East Timor and the New Humanitarian Interventionism," *International Affairs* (Royal Institute of International Affairs 1944–) 77, no. 4 (2001): 817.

[39] See Webster, "Non-State Diplomacy," 27; and James Cotton, *East Timor, Australia and Regional Order: Intervention and Its Aftermath in Southeast Asia* (London: RoutledgeCurzon, 2004).

"regional bully" against a peaceable "courageous underdog."[40] This "trauma drama" narrative, which began to be solidified in the 1980s with the Resistance's increased use of nonviolent forms of resistance and corresponding decreased use of violent forms of resistance, would have been disrupted at this pivotal moment in 1999 if Falintil had chosen to retaliate with force.

Human Rights and Politics

What does the Timor case tell us more generally about human rights and human rights activism? The Timor case gives the lie to various claims by scholars that human rights are either intrinsically apolitical or anti-revolutionary or have otherwise lost their ability to effect meaningful social or political change.[41] As we have seen, Timor's Resistance movement, as well as many, if not most, of the international solidarity groups that advocated for Timor, at least partially employed human rights discourses and practices in order to achieve the ultimate political end of Timorese independence.[42] Additionally, the use of human rights discourses to frame the Timorese conflict helped lead to concrete political outcomes in Timor. Timor would most likely not be independent today if its Resistance movement (and the international solidarity movement that supported the movement) had not employed human rights discourses and practices to frame its struggle for independence beginning in the 1980s and if human rights-based institutions such as the United Nations had not existed and acted in relation to Timor at critical moments. The effectiveness of the use of human rights discourses in the Timor case is evidenced by the fact that there was more violence, death, and suffering in Timor in the 1970s, immediately following the Indonesian invasion, than there was in the 1990s. Yet no action was taken on the part of the international community to intervene during that period when the violence was not framed in terms of human rights.

At the same time, the avowed or perceived apolitical nature of human rights is not irrelevant. Geoffrey Robinson has correctly noted that the Indonesian state authorities saw the use of human rights by Timorese as intrinsically political.[43] This included the use of human rights by Timor's Catholic Church. Still, the Indonesian state could not go to greater lengths to shut down the Church for speaking out on human rights issues because of the state's awareness that human rights discourses—particularly human rights discourses centered around suffering victimhood—are perceived, by the public at least, to be apolitical. They are perceived to be apolitical in that they are thought to be linked with questions of universal morality and ethics as opposed to questions of power, contestation, ideology, and governance. On a more concrete level, a human rights framing of the Timor conflict helped lead to Timorese independence by changing dominant representations of Timorese outside of Timor: third-world revolutionaries with

[40] David Webster, "Languages of Human Rights in Timor-Leste," *Asia Pacific: Perspectives* 11, no. 1 (2013): 16.

[41] Moyn, *The Last Utopia*, 43.

[42] Almost all the international solidarity groups that were active in the 1970s, and many of the groups that were active in the 1980s and the 1990s, supported Timor's independence movement. See Cotton, *East Timor, Australia and Regional Order*, 150. See also Annette Jansen, *Anti-Genocide Activists and the Responsibility to Protect* (London: Routledge, 2017), 32. Yet for different reasons, including the geopolitical climate discussed in this article, most of these groups focused primarily on issues of human rights during the 1980s, as opposed to the question of self-determination or independence.

[43] Robinson, "Human Rights History from the Ground Up," 34.

guns turned into unarmed human rights victims whom the international community had a moral responsibility to protect. These newer, seemingly apolitical representations of Timorese worked to gain the support and sympathy of internationals who had not been interested in or even aware of Timor's cause when the issue had been framed as one of anticolonialism. They also drew the support and sympathy of some who had actively opposed Timor's struggle when it had been framed in anticolonial terms.[44]

Human Rights and Agency

Why is it relevant *how* human rights discourses and practices worked to achieve the political goal of Timorese independence? Here I make another argument: while the use of depoliticizing human rights discourses in Timor's struggle for independence ultimately helped lead to Timor's independence, there has been an unanticipated side effect: the images consumed by the international community via media of "poor suffering Timorese" victims have served to obscure the immense agency of those Timorese involved in the production of these images.

A crucial point here is that members of Timor's Resistance were aware that that they were performing a drama for an international audience. Timor's Resistance movement obviously didn't create the two scenes of horrific violence discussed above, in which Timorese were killed and subjected to other human rights violations in massive numbers. Yet—and here I turn specifically to the violence on November 12, 1991—it was not entirely "accidental," random, or unexpected that this violence occurred and was caught on film.[45] My research has confirmed findings by others that Resistance leaders organized the demonstration on November 12 with the specific aim of creating Timorese victims for an international audience (although these same leaders were shocked and dismayed that the violence had been so great). A senior Falintil commander has described the Santa Cruz event as an "intentional sacrifice" to provoke a turning point externally and internally, noting "[i]t was the intention to create an incident in which many would be killed."[46] Another leader acknowledged that it was a human rights violation to sacrifice young people's lives, but said that the Resistance had "no options" at that time.[47] The foreign journalists who recorded the killings had connections to the Resistance and had been invited to the event by Resistance leaders; it is almost certain that there would have been no demonstration had these journalists not been present to record the resulting violence.

As Gregorio Sadhana, the leader of the demonstration on November 12 that led to the massacre, explained to me in 2012 (in relation to the event):

[44] A concrete example here concerns the Australian Bishop William Brennan and the Australian Catholic Social Justice Council. While they had previously defined themselves as "totally anti-Timorese," after the Santa Cruz massacre, they began to "sympathize . . . with the 'poor suffering Timorese.'" Quoted in Clinton Fernandes, *The Independence of East Timor: Multi-Dimensional Perspectives—Occupation, Resistance, and International Political Activism* (Portland, OR: Sussex Academic Press, 2011), 98.

[45] Webster, "Languages of Human Rights in Timor-Leste," 12.

[46] Quoted in John Braithwaite, Hilary Charlesworth, and Adérito Soares, *Networked Governance of Freedom and Tyranny: Peace in Timor-Leste* (Acton, AUS: ANU E Press, 2012); Braithwaite, Hilary Charlesworth, and Adérito Soares, *Networked Governance of Freedom and Tyranny*, 86.

[47] Quoted in Braithwaite, Charlesworth, and Soares, *Networked Governance of Freedom and Tyranny*, 86.

We did what? Prepared, organized, showed to the world that it is true that in Timor there are massacres. Things happened in Kraras; the world didn't say anything. Things happened in Jakarta Dua, in Ainaro, and other places, the world didn't say anything. We saw that we needed to do something that the world knew about. What could we do? Coordinate with foreign journalists so they would come, film it, and send it back overseas. . . . Prepare well, organize it, and send it out to the world so the world can see that it's true, in Timor there are massacres. Then the world would stand up.

Timorese were of course victimized by the brutal Indonesian regime. Yet, as this article has shown, and as Sadhana's quote emphasizes, Timorese also actively and agentively produced a narrative of victimhood for an international audience.[48] Of course, these realities are inextricably intertwined; among other things, the production of a narrative of victimhood at times involved the production of actual victims, as seen with the Santa Cruz case. Yet it was the narrative of victimhood—not the victimhood itself, or at least not the victimhood by itself—that ultimately won the attention and support of the international community. Too often this distinction has been overlooked and Timorese agency in creating a narrative of victimhood has been erased. One concrete outcome of this is that in the post-independence era former members of Timor's clandestine front—those most directly involved in employing human rights—have received less attention and valorization from Timor's state than former members of Falintil.[49]

Human Rights and Anticolonialism

My final argument is that the Timor case illustrates overlap between the movements or ideologies of anticolonialism and human rights (and between the right to self-determination and the rest of the human rights corpus). This point gains relevance when situated in the context of literature on the subject, in which the relationship between anticolonialism, the right to self-determination, and human rights is debated.

Various scholars have asserted that most, if not all, anticolonial movements (particularly those that occurred post-1948) were also human rights movements. Arguments include the following: anticolonial movements intentionally exploited reports about rights violations in order to win the support of international public opinion, anticolonial leaders explicitly referred to human rights in their arguments, and incidents brought to attention by human rights petitions limited the role of colonial

---

[48] A very different illustration of Timorese agency in producing a narrative of victimhood includes the following: a former clandestine member told me that in the post-Santa Cruz era when the Indonesians were "on their best behavior" (a result of the negative publicity the Indonesian regime had received post-massacre), clandestine members would occasionally stage and document fake human rights violations to keep the attention of the international community. This informant told me of an instance where members of the Resistance poured animal blood on themselves and took pictures. He also told me of instances where members of the clandestine movement, himself included, feigned injury in jail when the International Committee of the Red Cross (ICRC) came to visit.

[49] The failure to recognize the agency of Timorese clandestine members in producing a narrative of victimhood also accounts for the fact, as noted in the Introduction, that histories that examine the employment of human rights in Timor's independence struggle tend to focus on their use by Timor's Catholic Church or by the international solidarity front that supported Timor, as opposed to by Timor's Resistance movement itself (to the extent that histories do focus on the use of human rights by Timor's Resistance movement, they tend to focus on the use by Timor's external diplomatic front as opposed to by the internal fronts).

powers as credible actors.[50] A final argument is that anticolonial movements' use of human rights was not only strategic but that leaders and followers in the movements actually believed in human rights—they drew on and adhered to the ideas behind human rights.[51] Underlying these arguments is the claim that the inclusion of the right to self-determination in human rights documents—a right promoted by the newly independent African, Asian (and Arab) countries—represents a natural and logical pairing between self-determination and human rights.[52] The right to self-determination is the "prerequisite for fulfilling other rights aspirations."[53] It is the "right to have rights," or the "first right."[54]

Other scholars have critiqued these claims. Most famously, the historian Samuel Moyn has argued that the idea of anticolonial self-determination was based on the Rights of Man as proclaimed at the end of the 18th century, not on human rights, and that these two sets of rights are fundamentally different (as such, Moyn argues, human rights only emerged in the 1970s after the demise of the anticolonial project). In addition to arguing that human rights are mostly afforded to individuals, while self-determination is a group or collective right, Moyn argues—echoing discussions above—that the Rights of Man are political or revolutionary, whereas human rights are anti-revolutionary or apolitical.[55] Accordingly, Moyn asserts that anticolonial movements were not human rights movements; they were about nothing more than sovereignty and gaining freedom from the colonial masters.[56]

This article has already shown that Timorese successfully used human rights discourses to achieve the political end of independence (even if this political use of human rights involved a presentation of Timorese as apolitical victims). Moyn's assertion of a strict binary between human rights and self-determination, particularly in relation to the question of political efficacy, is thus challenged by the Timor case. However, here I assert a separate point. While some Timorese may have primarily employed human rights as a mere tool to achieve self-determination, without being ideologically bound to the larger human rights corpus and its ideals, others Timorese truly saw human

---

[50] Fabian Klose, "Debating Human Rights and Decolonization," *Imperial & Global Forum Blog*, February 18, 2014, https://imperialglobalexeter.com/2014/02/18/debating-human-rights-and-decolonization; Roland Burke, *Decolonization and the Evolution of International Human Rights* (Philadelphia: University of Pennsylvania Press, 2010); Klose, "Debating Human Rights and Decolonization."

[51] Bonny Ibhawoh, "Testing the Atlantic Charter: Linking Anticolonialism, Self-Determination and Universal Human Rights," *The International Journal of Human Rights* 18 (2014): 7–8.

[52] Burke, *Decolonization and the Evolution of International Human Rights*, 36.

[53] Ibhawoh, "Testing the Atlantic Charter," 7.

[54] Simpson, "Denying the 'First Right.'"

[55] Moyn also argues asserts another difference: he notes that the Rights of Man are granted by the state to its citizens, whereas human rights are afforded universally, based on the notion of a common and natural shared humanity. Moyn, *The Last Utopia*, 20–21.

[56] Moyn points out that postwar anticolonial activists rarely invoked the phrase "human rights" or appealed to the Universal Declaration of 1948. Even those few anticolonialists who did talk about human rights, after newly independent colonies had pushed the international community to include self-determination in the idea of human rights in the 1960s only meant self-determination, and self-determination was still linked to nothing more than gaining independence. Moyn, *The Last Utopia*, 85–119. Jan Eckel concurs that postwar anticolonial activists rarely invoked the phrase "human rights" or appealed to the Universal Declaration of 1948. He also asserts that human rights accusations "never formed a dominant motivation for colonial retreat." Eckel, "Human Rights and Decolonization," 115, 129.

rights and self-determination as linked and were fighting for both at the same time. In other words, at least some Timorese believed the argument that the Resistance directed at the international community—that Timorese self-determination was necessary for Timorese to attain basic human rights. For many Timorese, the fulfillment of individual human rights became a true goal or end in and of itself, alongside self-determination. Relevant here is that it was the violence of the Indonesian regime that brought so many younger Timorese (and Timor's Church) to support Timor's Resistance movement in the first place. Also relevant is that the degree of the brutality of the Indonesian regime in Timor was, by all accounts, a result of the illegitimacy of Indonesian rule. As Benedict Anderson pointed out in his article on the formation of Timorese national identity: "the use of aerial bombardments, the napalming of villages, the systematic herding of people into resettlement centers . . . [had] no real counterparts in Indonesian government policy toward, as it were, 'real Indonesians.'"[57]

Conclusion

Timor's Resistance movement began to increasingly employ human rights discourses and practices in the 1980s to win the attention and support of the major Western powers, which had begun to decreasingly devalue anticolonial struggles and increasingly value struggles for human rights. Timorese in the movement appealed to the catastrophe prevention mission of the human rights regime. They used human rights discourses and practices—including the practice of nonviolent resistance—to represent themselves to Western audiences as innocent victims whom the international community had a moral responsibility to protect. While Timor's legal claim to independence was based on Indonesia's denial of Timor's right to self-determination upon its invasion of Timor in 1975, it was this deployment of a human rights narrative that ultimately won Timor its independence.

The Timor case has broader lessons to teach us about the use of human rights in struggles for social and political change. It provides an example of human rights being successfully used as a political tool to contest unequal power relations (and achieve the overtly political ends of self-determination and sovereignty). The Timor case also illustrates a paradox at the heart of a certain kind of human rights activism. While human rights discourses and practices were successfully used by Timorese to achieve the political goal of independence, they were able to have the effect they did because of their perceived apoliticality. One problematic outcome of this perceived apoliticality—or of the depoliticizing effects of human rights discourse—has been an obscuring of the agency of Timorese who employed human rights to help to construct a narrative of Timorese victimhood. Finally, the Timor case shows us that there is significant overlap between anticolonialism and human rights (or between the right-to-self-determination and the rest of the human rights corpus). Beyond the reality that human rights were successfully deployed in Timor to win Timorese independence, it is fair to argue that many Timorese truly believed they were fighting for independence and human rights at the same time, without seeing in this any contradiction.

---

[57] Benedict Anderson, "Imagining 'East Timor,'" *Arena Magazine (Fitzroy, Vic)* 4 (1993): 25.

Keeping the Issue Alive: TAPOL and the International Campaign for Self-Determination and Justice in East Timor

Hannah Loney

> An Indonesian takeover of "Portuguese" East Timor would bring bloodshed and terror to the country, as did the military takeover in Indonesia in 1965 . . . TAPOL will continue to do all it can to alert world opinion to the seriousness of this situation and to monitor as far as is possible developments in Timor, in particular in the event of an Indonesian takeover.[1]

From 1974, as Portugal commenced decolonization processes in East Timor and the Indonesian military prepared to invade the territory, TAPOL, the British Campaign for the Release of Indonesian Political Prisoners, was one of the few international organizations to warn of the humanitarian tragedy that would ensue. The invasion occurred on December 7, 1975, with the predicted consequences. Upon its founding in 1973, TAPOL had focused on the plight of political prisoners (*tahanan politik* or *tapol*) in Indonesia, mostly held without trial as suspected Communists following the violent transition to the New Order regime in 1965–66. In 1980, TAPOL expanded its mandate to focus on victims of all forms of oppression in Indonesia and East Timor, changing its name to TAPOL, the British Campaign for the Defence of Political Prisoners and Human Rights in Indonesia and from 1986, to TAPOL, the Indonesia Human Rights

Hannah Loney (PhD Melbourne) is an expert in women's and gender history and 20th c. Southeast Asian history, currently Visiting Associate Professor at the Central European University (Vienna, Austria)

[1] "East Timor: Indonesian Takeover Means Bloodshed and Terror," *TAPOL Bulletin* 12, October 1975, p. 1.

Campaign.[2] Throughout the Indonesian occupation of East Timor (1975–99), TAPOL fervently advocated for the human rights of the East Timorese people by organizing rallies, workshops, and speaking tours; publishing regular bulletins and pamphlets; and supporting the activities of other international solidarity groups. The regular *TAPOL Bulletin*, in particular, was one of the key ways in which the organization assisted in keeping the issue of East Timor alive.

This article explores the role, activities, and influence of TAPOL in the international campaign for self-determination and justice in East Timor. It draws primarily on the *TAPOL Bulletin* (which was published from 1973 to 2008),[3] alongside extant documents from the organization, to trace the tactics that TAPOL used to rally support for the East Timor issue, how these changed over time and in accordance with broader historical processes and events. The bulletin contained interviews, news updates, and analyses on East Timor and was instrumental in influencing public opinion on the issue in Britain and beyond. It also drew uniquely on Indonesian language sources, including captured Indonesian military documents, as well as radio broadcasts from inside occupied East Timor, Catholic Church sources, and personal testimony. With approximately nine hundred subscribers and distributed across seventy-five countries in Europe, America, the Pacific, Australia, and Indonesia,[4] the bulletin positioned TAPOL as a leading member of the international campaign that was eventually successful in securing self-determination for East Timor. Following the independence referendum in 1999, TAPOL continued to advocate for redress for human rights violations that were committed during the occupation and to monitor political developments in the independent state. It was this ongoing concern that firmly solidified TAPOL's status as a key organization committed to securing peace and justice in an independent East Timor.

Looking at the role and activities of one key activist organization provides a new approach to analyzing the Indonesian occupation of East Timor. There are relatively few sustained studies of the East Timor solidarity movement and transnational political activism, with the exception of important work by Brad Simpson, Clinton Fernandes, and David Webster.[5] Simpson, for example, examines the emergence and growth of an East Timor solidarity movement in the United States. In so doing, he demonstrates the crucial role played by transnational solidarity networks in maintaining East Timor's visibility internationally and in pressuring the Indonesian government to allow a referendum on the territory's future in 1999. Indeed, Simpson argues that "in few other contemporary struggles for international justice have such networks played

---

[2] TAPOL, "About Us," accessed February 28, 2023, http://www.tapol.org/about-us.

[3] The *TAPOL Bulletin* has been digitized and is available online via Victoria University's (Melbourne, Australia) Research Repository: https://vuir.vu.edu.au. Other TAPOL archival material, including the Occasional Report Series, is also available online via the *Timor International Solidarity Archive (TiSA)*: https://timorarchive.com/tapol.

[4] Katharine McGregor, "The Making of a Transnational Activist: The Indonesian Human Rights Campaigner Carmel Budiardjo," in *The Transnational Activist: Transformations and Comparisons from the Anglo-World Since the Nineteenth Century*, ed. Stefan Berge and Sean Scalmer (Cham: Palgrave-Macmillan, 2017).

[5] Brad Simpson, "Solidarity in an Age of Globalization: The Transnational Movement for East Timor and U.S. Foreign Policy," *Peace and Change* 29, no. 3/4 (July 2004): 453–82; Clinton Fernandes, *The Independence of East Timor: Multi-Dimensional Perspectives—Occupation, Resistance, and International Political Activism* (Eastbourne, UK: Sussex Academic Press, 2011); David Webster, Juliana Brito Santana Leal, and Fernando Jorge Saraiva Ferreira Jr., "Putting Timor on the Global Agenda in 1985: Solidarity Activism Ten Years After Indonesia's Invasion of East Timor," *Indonesia* 107 (April 2019): 3–15.

as prominent a role in bringing about meaningful political change as in East Timor."[6] For Fernandes, the work of overseas scholars and activists—who enlisted influential constituencies in their respective political, media, and religious spheres—were crucial in creating a "structure of legitimacy" around the East Timor issue, which was eventually successful in pressuring the Indonesian government to act in 1999.[7] Webster has examined transnational solidarity activism after 1985; a year that became a "mobilizing moment" for the transnational solidarity network.[8] There are brief statements that attest to TAPOL's valuable contribution to the East Timor solidarity movement, for instance, in the final report of the Commission for Reception, Truth, and Reconciliation in Timor-Leste (Comissão de Acolhimento, Verdade e Reconciliação de Timor Leste, CAVR).[9] However, there is no sustained study of TAPOL's activism on the East Timor issue.

This article traces the role of TAPOL in building support for the East Timor issue in Britain, as well as its interaction with a transnational solidarity movement in support of self-determination for East Timor. It positions this discussion within the context of transnational political activism and solidarity networks, which were driven by East Timor's campaign for national self-determination. It considers the extent to which international forces, particularly powerful Western governments, such as the British government, and institutions of global governance, such as the United Nations, responded to this movement. In so doing, it reveals some of the intersections between the local and the global, particularly within the broader international context of the Cold War.

Decolonization and Invasion: A Brief History of the Conflict

East Timor, a small half-island at the eastern end of the Indonesian archipelago, was colonized by the Portuguese in the sixteenth century. Following the Carnation Revolution on April 25, 1974, Portugal initiated decolonization processes in its overseas territories, including Portuguese Timor. Political associations formed rapidly, distinguished by different visions for the future of the territory. Almost immediately, the most popular party was the Revolutionary Front for an Independent East Timor (Frente Revolucionária de Timor-Leste Independente, FRETILIN), which advocated for immediate independence from Portuguese colonial rule. After a brief conflict erupted between the major parties, FRETILIN emerged victorious. It subsequently began to implement its plans for the rapid transformation and development of East Timorese society and politics, in accordance with the principles of anticolonial nationalism, unity, and immediate independence.[10] International observers in the territory at the time reported that FRETILIN was in

---

[6] Simpson, "Solidarity in the Age of Globalization," 453–54.

[7] Fernandes, *The Independence of East Timor*, 49.

[8] Webster et al., "Putting Timor on the Global Agenda," 4.

[9] The Timor-Leste Commission for Reception, Truth, and Reconciliation (CAVR), *Chega! The Final Report of the Timor-Leste Commission for Reception, Truth and Reconciliation (CAVR)* (Jakarta: KPG in cooperation with STP-CAVR, 2013), 713.

[10] Frente Revolucionária do Timor Leste Independente (Revolutionary Front for an Independent East Timor), "Program of the Revolutionary Front of Independent East Timor (Fretilin)," in *What Is Fretilin? The Revolutionary Front for an Independent East Timor (Fretilin) Explains Its Aims in a Question and Answer Format* (Sydney: Campaign for Independent East Timor, Sydney, 1974).

effective control, that the party was rapidly gaining popular support, and that a peaceful transfer of power to the FRETILIN administration was possible.[11]

The government of the Republic of Indonesia, however, made clear its designs for East Timor once Portugal had signaled its intention to leave. The official position, as outlined by Indonesia's Foreign Minister, Adam Malik, was that Indonesia had no intention to expand its territory and that it respected East Timor's right to self-determination.[12] At the same time, Indonesian military heads, such as Ali Murtopo, held talks in Lisbon and advocated for East Timor to "integrate" into Indonesia.[13] For the Indonesian administration, East Timor was not a viable economic entity and posed a threat to Indonesian national security. With Indonesian military operations on the border intensifying and a full-scale invasion looking increasingly imminent, FRETILIN became desperate to find a way to engage the international community. Thus, on November 28, 1975, FRETILIN unilaterally declared the independence of the Democratic Republic of Timor-Leste.[14] Indonesia's response was to facilitate the signing of the Balibo Declaration the following day in Kupang, West Timor, integrating East Timor into Indonesia.[15] Meanwhile, Indonesian troops were preparing to invade.

On December 7, 1975, Indonesia launched a full-scale land, sea, and air invasion of Dili. The invasion involved a large number of troops and was conducted under the pretext of "maintaining order."[16] For the next twenty-four years, the Republic of Indonesia occupied East Timor. During this time, the territory was run essentially as a military fiefdom by the Indonesian National Armed Forces (Angkatan Bersenjata Republik Indonesia, ABRI). The final report of the CAVR found that mass human rights violations were perpetrated throughout the period by the Indonesian military and their auxiliaries, including civilian killings and disappearance; forced displacement and famine; detention, torture, and ill-treatment; and sexual violence.[17] The United Nations (UN) formally recognized Portugal as the rightful ruler of East Timor up until the independence referendum in 1999.

[11] See, for example, Jill Jolliffe, *Report from East Timor* (Canberra: A. N. U. Student's Association, 1975); Helen Hill, *The Timor Story* (Melbourne: Timor Information Services, 1975); Roger East, *Independence or Death!: East Timor's Border War: Eye-Witness Reports* (Sydney: Campaign for Independent East Timor, 1975); and ACFOA Timor Task Force, *Report on Visit to East Timor for ACFOA Timor Task Force* (Canberra: Australian Council for Overseas Aid, 1975).

[12] Adam Malik, letter to José Ramos-Horta, Jakarta, June 17, 1974, *East Timor Law and Justice Bulletin*, October 29, 2016, http://www.easttimorlawandjusticebulletin.com/2016/10/17-june-1974-letter-from-indonesian.html.

[13] J. A. Ford, "Timor: Indonesia's Reluctant Takeover," British Embassy in Jakarta, Confidential Dispatch printed by the Foreign and Commonwealth Office for General (but Confidential) Distribution, Diplomatic Report No. 182/76," March 15, 1976, *The National Security Archive*, https://nsarchive2.gwu.edu//NSAEBB/indexuk.htm#doc25.

[14] Democratic Republic of East Timor (RDTL), "Texto da Declaração Unilateral da Independência de Timor-Leste, Proclamada pela FRETILIN em 28 de Novembro de 1975" (Text of the Unilateral Declaration of Timor-Leste's independence, proclaimed by FRETILIN on 28 November 1975).

[15] "Joint Declaration by APODETI, UDT, KOTA and the Partido Trabilhista, Issued at Batugade, 30 November 1975," in *East Timor and the International Community: Basic Documents*, ed. Heiki Krieger (Cambridge: Cambridge University Press, 1997), 40.

[16] H. E. Mr. Ali Alatas, Minister for Foreign Affairs of Indonesia, "East Timor: De-Bunking the Myths Around a Process of Decolonization: Remarks by H. E. Mr. Ali Alatas, Minister for Foreign Affairs of Indonesia, before Members of the National Press Club, Washington, D.C., 20 February 1992," in Krieger, *East Timor and the International Community*, 277.

[17] CAVR, *Chega!*.

From the onset, it was the British government's policy to distance itself from the East Timor issue, essentially to reduce the possibility of public pressure to condemn Indonesia. While acknowledging that the East Timorese were being denied their right to self-determination and never recognizing the Jakarta regime in the territory as legitimate, successive British governments provided tacit support for Indonesia's efforts to incorporate the territory.[18] Based on its low-profile policy, the British government abstained from all UN General Assembly Resolutions on the question of East Timor between 1975 and 1982, while supporting two weaker Security Council Resolutions that recognized East Timor's right to self-determination and calling on the Indonesian government to withdraw its troops.[19] At the same time, the British government continued to pursue its commercial and industrial interests, including maintaining a significant aid and military cooperation program, with Indonesia.[20]

Thus, while outwardly proclaiming to support East Timor's right to self-determination, the provision of military aid by a major Western power and member of the UN Security Council was a signal of substantial political support for Indonesia's annexation of the territory. In fact, for the East Timorese independence activist José Ramos-Horta, Britain was "the single worst obstructionist of any industrialized country" to East Timor's struggle.[21] Despite this difficult environment in Britain, two civil society organizations took up the issue of East Timor early on: the British Campaign for an Independent East Timor (BCIET), which was founded in 1974, and TAPOL, which had been established in 1973 by Carmel Budiardjo, a British woman who had been imprisoned in Indonesia during the anti-Communist crackdowns in 1965–66.[22] Budiardjo and her colleague Liem Soei Liong, an Indonesian activist living in exile in the Netherlands (and whose human rights activism is noted in Pocut Hanifah's article on the intersections between the Indonesian and East Timor solidarity movements in this special issue), were the driving force behind TAPOL's campaigning. The work of these two organizations, alongside the later work of church agencies and several distinguished patrons, made Britain, in time, a "key international support centre" for the international campaign for the independence of East Timor.[23]

The Situation Unfolds: TAPOL's Early Involvement in the East Timor Issue

TAPOL's early coverage of Indonesia's impending invasion of East Timor and predictions of the devastation that would ensue was indicative of the attentiveness and thoroughness

---

[18] CAVR, *Chega!*, pp. 651–56.

[19] General Assembly Resolution 3485, 12 December 1975; Resolution 31/53, 1 December 1976; Resolution 32/34, 28 November 1977; Resolution 33/39, 13 December 1978; Resolution 34/40, 21 November 1979; Resolution 35/27, 11 November 1980; Resolution 36/50, 24 November 1981; and Resolution 37/30, 23 November 1982. S/RES/384 (1975), Adopted by the Security Council at its 1869th meeting on 22 December 1975; and S/RES/389 (1976), Adopted by the Security Council at its 1914th meeting on 22 April 1976.

[20] TAPOL, Indonesian Human Rights Campaign, 'Ethics, Investments and Repression–Britain and Indonesia: The Test for Government and Business', TAPOL, London, 31 March 1998.

[21] Cited in John Gittins, 'Horta Accuses Britain of Blocking Action on Indonesia', *The Guardian*, 17 June 1992.

[22] CAVR, *Chega!*, p. 712. For an analysis of Budiardjo's life and activism, see McGregor, 'The Making of a Transnational Activist'. For a first-hand account, see Carmel Budiardjo, *Surviving Indonesia's Gulag*, Cassell, London, 1996.

[23] CAVR, *Chega!*, 712–13.

with which the organization approached the issue in subsequent decades. In its regular bulletin, TAPOL covered preparations for the invasion from as early as March 1975. In August 1975, TAPOL wrote a letter to the British government, urging it to "work for an international solution that would safeguard the right to self-determination of the Timorese people." The letter recalled "the massacres and repression that had followed in the wake of military rule in Indonesia" in 1965–66 and warned of similar "bloodshed and terror" that would ensue in East Timor.[24] The invasion took place four months later, with the expected and devastating consequences for the East Timorese.

TAPOL's attention to the East Timor issue arose primarily out of concern for human rights and the humanitarian tragedy that was unfolding, and its focus was for the most part concerned with these issues. For more general political developments in the territory, the organization initially relied on the coverage of the BCIET and for which TAPOL allocated space within its regular bulletin. In the early years of the occupation, TAPOL was one of a small number of solidarity organizations in Europe and Australia that campaigned on the issue of self-determination for East Timor. TAPOL aimed to keep its readers abreast of developments within the territory that were, by contrast, "almost totally ignored in the world press."[25] After the virtual defeat of FRETILIN's armed wing, the Armed Forces for the National Liberation of East Timor (Forças Armadas da Libertação Nacional de Timor-Leste, FALINTIL) in 1979, international solidarity waned and many groups disbanded, including the BCIET. Carmel Budiardjo later described the following decade as "the bleakest period for East Timor internationally," noting that the prospect of independence for East Timor at this time seemed "very remote."[26] In contrast to many other solidarity organizations that fell by the wayside, and in light of the release of many political prisoners in Indonesia related to the 1965 case, in 1979, TAPOL decided to focus more extensively on human rights in East Timor.

TAPOL's early activism was thus aimed at informing its readers about the situation in East Timor and in cultivating international support for the issue, with the additional aim of effecting policy changes on the part of Western governments toward Indonesia. That East Timor was closed off from the outside world from 1976 meant international solidarity networks were particularly important in sharing and disseminating rare information from inside the territory. TAPOL drew early parallels between the methods used by the Indonesian military in the wake of 1965–66, which, it argued, laid the foundations for the system of repression that characterized the occupation of East Timor. An article written by Julie Southwood in a 1980 bulletin, for example, summarized the preliminary results of TAPOL's research into Indonesian political trials. Southwood claimed that the notion of a "communist threat" had been used to justify Indonesia's invasion of East Timor, which would not have been effective had it not been for the September 30 Movement (*Pengkhianatan G30S/PKI*, G30S/PKI) theory.[27]

---

[24] "East Timor: Indonesian Takeover Means Bloodshed and Terror," *TAPOL Bulletin* 12, October 1975, 1.

[25] "Spotlight on the Massacres," *TAPOL Bulletin* 15, April 1976, 1.

[26] Carmel Budiardjo, "The International Solidarity Movement for East Timor: A Weapon More Powerful than Guns," May 17, 2002, TAPOL: *Promoting Human Rights, Peace and Democracy in Indonesia*, http://tapol.org/news-and-reports/news/international-solidarity-movement-east-timor-weapon-more-powerful-guns.

[27] Julie Southwood, "Indonesia's Political Trials: 'Legal' Dimensions of a Continuing Tragedy," *TAPOL Bulletin* 37, January 1980, 15. On the September 30 movement and its aftereffects in Indonesia, see John Roosa, *Pretext for Mass Murder: The September 30th Movement and Suharto's Coup d'état in Indonesia* (Madison: University of

In accordance with this link, a large portion of TAPOL's April 1976 bulletin featured recently received documents on the 1965–66 violence. The editor explained the purpose of this coverage was to "impress on our readers the gravity of the present situation in East Timor" and to "help them [readers] gain a better understanding of the way in which Indonesia's present system of repression was born."[28] In the August 1977 bulletin, in recognition of the upcoming twelfth anniversary of the September 30 movement, TAPOL announced a major intensification of its East Timor campaign by expanding its research and advocacy. TAPOL made this commitment not only to highlight the recently announced mass transfer of Indonesian political prisoners to labor camps, but also to "help draw the attention of the world to what is happening in East Timor, where Indonesia's war of conquest drags on to the accompaniment of murder, torture, frequent rapes and, of course detention of civilians without trial."[29] Drawing parallels between the 1965 case and the occupation of East Timor was thus a strategy utilized by TAPOL to highlight the continuity of military violence under the New Order regime, as well as the ongoing complicity of the international community.

Similar to other international solidarity organizations, TAPOL pieced together information about events inside East Timor that it gleaned from a range of different sources, including reports from foreign journalists and ambassadors who were permitted access to the territory for special occasions. For example, it drew on observations made by a delegation of ambassadors and journalists that visited select areas of East Timor in the late 1970s. They observed the incarceration of large numbers of people into camps and the "desperate circumstances" in which they lived. In response, TAPOL appealed for its readers to campaign for the International Red Cross to be given "unlimited access to all parts of East Timor," so that it could assess the situation and carry out much needed humanitarian work.[30] Information was also provided to the organization via Radio Maubere, the East Timorese resistance's only direct link to the outside world after the Indonesian military closed off the territory, until it was captured by the Indonesian military in November 1978.[31] Broadcasts from inside East Timor were picked up in Darwin, Australia, and disseminated by the Denis Freney-led Campaign for an Independent East Timor (CIET) to FRETILIN representatives abroad, the UN, support groups, the media, and governments.

Other information was gleaned from reports or letters written by Catholic priests, which were smuggled out of the territory and then published in the international press, especially in Australian news outlets. These reports were often extremely critical of the Indonesian military's conduct in East Timor. A letter written in October 1977 by a Catholic priest, for example, accused the Indonesian military of overseeing a "barbarous genocide of innocent people" within the territory.[32] Interviews with East Timorese

---

Wisconsin Press, 2006); and Katharine McGregor, Jess Melvin, and Annie Pohlman, *The Indonesian Genocide of 1965: Causes, Dynamics and Legacies* (Cham: Palgrave Macmillan, 2018).

[28] "Spotlight on the Massacres," *TAPOL Bulletin* 15, April 1976, 1.

[29] "New Tasks for the 13th Year," *TAPOL Bulletin* 23, August 1977, 1.

[30] "Starvation Camps in East Timor," *TAPOL Bulletin* 30, October 1978, 1.

[31] For more on the radio link, see Rob Wesley-Smith, "Radio Maubere and Links to East Timor," *Free East Timor: Australia's Culpability in East Timor's Genocide*, ed. Jim Aubrey (Milson's Point: Random House Australia, 1998), 83–102.

[32] "Letter from East Timor," *TAPOL Bulletin* 28, June 1978, 12.

refugees in Lisbon by James Dunn, Australia's former Consul in Dili, also provided information about life inside the territory and were published in the bulletin.[33] These accounts broadly confirmed reports provided by FRETILIN via the radio link: killings, massacres, prison camps, and the systematic and sustained use of torture and detention. TAPOL also traced the issue of the five television journalists—two of whom were British subjects—working for Australian news publications when, in October 1975, they were killed at the border town of Balibo.[34] This issue grew to become emblematic of Western governments' complicity in Indonesia's invasion and annexation of East Timor.[35] Despite these reports many Western governments, including the British and the Australian, maintained or even increased their aid programs to Indonesia, thus provoking vehement opposition from organizations such as TAPOL.

In addition to updates in its regular bulletin, TAPOL collaborated with other London-based organizations to sponsor demonstrations and seminars on the East Timor issue. They also screened films and organized discussions about the situation in the territory. TAPOL also sought to influence the British government's policy toward Indonesia and to limit its financial and military support for the Indonesian military. In 1978, for example, TAPOL launched a campaign in collaboration with the BCIET and the Campaign Against Arms Trade (CAAT), a UK-based organization working to end the international arms trade, to stop the recently announced sale of British Aerospace Hawk ground attack/trainers to the Indonesian government and to impose an embargo on all future sales. TAPOL declared that the sale contradicted the British government's "avowed concern for human rights considerations in its approval of arms exports," as the jets would result in more civilian casualties in East Timor.[36] As part of this campaign, TAPOL printed and distributed thousands of leaflets, wrote to members of Parliament, and solicited the assistance of bulletin readers to act. TAPOL also protested the British government's decision to cancel Indonesia's debts arising from past economic assistance. TAPOL wrote to Judith Hart, Minister for Overseas Development, protesting this financial concession to Indonesia, in addition to the proposed sale of the eight Hawk ground attack/trainer aircraft, on the grounds of "Indonesia's deplorable record of human rights violations."[37] When the number of planes to be sold increased from eight to sixteen in late 1978, TAPOL's campaign against arms sales to Indonesia intensified and continued throughout the Indonesian occupation.

Keeping the Issue Alive: TAPOL's Campaign Intensifies

Following the release of many political prisoners in Indonesia in 1979 related to the 1965 case, TAPOL refined its agenda, asserting that human rights campaigning on behalf of political prisoners in Indonesia was still necessary. In fact, it was necessary "to work just as hard or even harder" to advocate for the release of political prisoners and especially

[33] "Massacres and Tortures in East Timor," *TAPOL Bulletin* 20, February 1977, 1.

[34] "Foreign Journalists Killed in Timor," *TAPOL Bulletin* 27, April 1978, 6.

[35] For more on the Balibo Five, see Desmond Ball and Hamish McDonald, *Death in Balibo Lies in Canberra* (St Leonards: Allen & Unwin, 2000); and Jill Jolliffe, *Cover-Up: The Story of the Balibo Five* (Carlton North: Scribe, 2001).

[36] "No Warplanes for Indonesia," *TAPOL Bulletin* 27, April 1978, 1.

[37] "Tapol Protest to British Government," *TAPOL Bulletin* 29, August 1978, 5.

to agitate in response to "the grotesque situation in East Timor where annexation by Indonesia has left a ghastly trail of death, starvation and large-scale incarceration."[38] This agenda was particularly significant given the recent disbandment of the BCIET. According to Carmel Budiardjo, it was now up to TAPOL to "keep the issue [of East Timor] alive" in Britain.[39] TAPOL's regular bulletin continued to provide updates on the human rights situation in East Timor, publishing extracts from reports provided by human rights organizations, such as Amnesty International and the Australia-based Action for World Development, as well as interviews with Church figures, such as Monsignor Martinho da Costa Lopes, the Apostolic Administrator in East Timor.[40]

TAPOL was increasingly able to use information provided by the Catholic Church, as well as other Catholic organizations, in its campaigning. Indeed, Michael Leach's article in this special issue demonstrates the significance of the Catholic Church to East Timorese independence campaign more broadly. For TAPOL, Church sources became particularly important after the appointment of Bishop Monsignor Carlos Filipe Ximenes Belo to the Dili Diocese in 1983, a move that strengthened resistance from the Catholic Church to the Indonesian occupation. In an open letter from 1984, reprinted in the bulletin, Belo appealed to the world: "Open your eyes to the brutalities of Indonesia."[41] A number of British-based Church organizations also began to take up the campaign in the 1980s, including the Catholic Institute for International Relations (CIIR) and the Catholic Agency for Overseas Development (CIOD). Significantly, in November 1983, the Indonesian Bishops' Conference sent an open letter to the Catholic Church in East Timor expressing sympathy and friendship with the people of East Timor "who are being deluged by most bitter trials both physically and spiritually."[42] As TAPOL noted in its commentary, the letter marked "an important turning point for the Indonesian Catholic Church, the first time it has publicly expressed concern for the situation in East Timor."[43] This reflection demonstrates the organization's capacity to critically comment on developments within the territory and to recognize the expanding scope of solidarity for East Timor.

During the 1980s, letters from inside the territory and interviews with refugees continued to provide TAPOL with valuable information, including firsthand accounts of life inside the territory. On September 18, 1982, for example, TAPOL interviewed Carlos Afonso, an East Timorese refugee in Perth, Australia, about his life in Dili. Through his job as a clerk at the Regional Assembly, Afonso testified that he had seen "and heard about many things, murders, rapes, crimes, everything."[44] One of the unique features of TAPOL's coverage, however, was the inclusion of translated Indonesian military

---

[38] "TAPOL Campaign Intensified," *TAPOL Bulletin* 32, February 1979, 1.

[39] Carmel Budiardjo, "The International Solidarity Movement for East Timor."

[40] "Human Rights Violations in East Timor" (Report by the Australian Organization, Action for World Development), *TAPOL Bulletin* 36, October 1979, 4; "The Disappeared" (Based on a Report Issued by Amnesty International), *TAPOL Bulletin* 39, May 1980, 1; "Interview with Former Bishop of East Timor," *TAPOL Bulletin* 59, September 1983, 3–8.

[41] "Appeal to the World from the Bishop of Dili: 'Open Your Eyes to the Brutality of Indonesia,'" *TAPOL Bulletin* 63, May 1984, 1.

[42] "Indonesian Bishops' Open Letter to East Timor Church," *TAPOL Bulletin* 62, March 1984, 14.

[43] "Indonesian Bishops' Open Letter," 14.

[44] "East Timorese Refugee Interviewed by TAPOL," *TAPOL Bulletin* 54, November 1982, 15.

documents. A special supplement in the July 1983 bulletin, for example, featured military instructions to Indonesian troops in East Timor that had been captured by resistance forces on December 30, 1982.[45] Translated extracts from Indonesian newspapers, such as *Tempo, Kompas, Merdeka, Jakarta Post*, and *Suara Pembaruan*, also provided unique insights into Indonesian perspectives on life inside the occupied territory. Where possible, reports written by members of the resistance were also reproduced in the bulletin. For example, occasional reports written by the resistance leader, Xanana Gusmão, were published, detailing lists of persons massacred, disappeared, imprisoned, and tortured.[46] A number of foreign representatives who visited the territory for special occasions from the 1980s also reported to TAPOL on the deplorable human rights situation.[47]

In addition, TAPOL traced developments on the East Timor issue in the international diplomatic arena. For example, the bulletin reported on developments from the annual UN Human Rights Commission, the UN Decolonization Committee (more formally known as the Special Committee on the Situation with Regard to the Implementation of the Declaration on the Granting of Independence to Colonial Countries and Peoples), the UN General Assembly, and the UN Sub-Committee on the Prevention of Discrimination and Protection of Minorities. TAPOL representatives, in particular Carmel Budiardjo and Liem Soei Liong, joined activists and human rights organizations from all over the world to testify throughout the 1980s and 1990s on behalf of East Timor at these hearings. TAPOL staff also submitted joint petitions with other organizations and individuals to the UN. TAPOL reported to its members on this activism in the bulletin and in a new series of supplements on human rights and the military occupation of East Timor: the Occasional Report Series.[48] The coverage paid close attention also to the position of the Portuguese government on the question of East Timor and to the annual UN-sponsored talks between Portugal and Indonesia to try to find a peaceful solution to the issue.

However, it was TAPOL's campaign for an arms embargo against Indonesia that won widespread support in Britain: "Don't trade with mass murderers," read the headline on the front page of the November 1981 bulletin.[49] On this point, TAPOL's aim was to exert pressure on the British government to stop aiding and abetting the Indonesian military regime, either by supplying equipment to its armed forces or by providing economic aid. From April 1978, TAPOL campaigned ceaselessly against British arms sales to Indonesia, in alliance with other UK organizations and several distinguished patrons. These patrons

[45] Special Supplement, *TAPOL Bulletin* 58, July 1983.

[46] "Fretilin Report on Human Rights Abuses," *TAPOL Bulletin* 78, December 1986, 15–19.

[47] See, for example, a report by Anders Uhlin, a Swedish tourist, who visited the territory from May to November 1989 and whose observations were reproduced in the bulletin. "Impressions of West Papua and East Timor," *TAPOL Bulletin* 97, February 1990, 11.

[48] TAPOL Occasional Report No. 1: Exchange of Messages with Fretilin; No. 2: UDT-Fretilin Joint Statement; No. 4: TAPOL Statement on East Timor to the UN Decolonization Committee, August 1986; No. 5: The 1987 Indonesian Election in East Timor; No. 6: TAPOL Statement on East Timor to the UN Decolonization Committee, August 1987; No. 9: TAPOL Statement on East Timor to the UN Committee of 24, August 1988, No. 11: TAPOL Statement to the UN Decolonization Committee, August 1990; No. 13: TAPOL's Statement to the UN Decolonization Committee, August 1990; No. 15: TAPOL Statement to the 1991 Meeting of the UN Decolonization Committee; No. 19: TAPOL's Statement to the UN Decolonization Committee, New York, July 1992; No. 22: TAPOL's Statement to the UN Decolonization Committee, New York, July 1993.

[49] "Don't Trade with Mass Murderers," *TAPOL Bulletin* 48, November 1981, 1.

included Lord Avebury of the Liberal Party, who also chaired the All-Party Parliamentary Group on Human Rights and served as TAPOL's Honorary President. Indeed, Lord Avebury became one of the most ardent supporters of the East Timor issue. In 1988, for example, TAPOL supported Lord Avebury's efforts to set up Parliamentarians for East Timor, an organization that repeatedly called for an arms embargo against Indonesia because of its occupation of East Timor. In 1989 a Labour MP, Ann Clwyd, visited East Timor and became another advocate for East Timor.[50] TAPOL collaborated with these two important public figures, repeatedly demanding that the British government "Stop all arms sales to Indonesia without delay!"[51] TAPOL called on readers to write to local MPs protesting the arms deal and organized demonstrations in support of this issue. One such demonstration took place outside the British Aerospace Annual General Meeting at a hotel in central London on April 26, 1984.[52] The arms issue peaked in January 1996, when four women entered a British Aerospace military site armed with hammers and disarmed a Hawk jet being readied for Indonesia.[53] Their trial made legal history when the judge acquitted them on the basis that they had acted in order to prevent a greater crime: the crime of genocide. The acquittal made headline news and attracted intense public debate and attention in the UK, elevating the arms embargo issue to a new level.[54]

Another form of advocacy utilized by TAPOL was to write public letters to members of the British Parliament and to compare the arms deals with Indonesia with other aspects of British foreign policy. On April 7, 1982, for example, Carmel Budiardjo wrote a letter to the Right Honourable Francis Pym, MP, the new Foreign and Commonwealth Secretary, in which she implored him to cease military sales to Indonesia in accordance with his decision to mobilize support to halt the Argentinian aggression. "Do you not agree that there is a paradox between what the British Government is calling upon others to do and what it has failed to do to stop the Indonesian aggressors?," Budiardjo wrote.[55] The issue of arms deals with Indonesia continued to attract attention not only within the UK, but across the globe. On September 29, 1983, TAPOL was among several organizations from the UK, Holland, Germany, Sweden, and Portugal that signed a statement that called on Western governments to "Stop arms exports to Indonesia! Suspend economic aid to Indonesian aggressors! Support the people of East Timor!"[56] Increases in the export of arms to Indonesia from Britain, however, still went ahead despite the efforts of organizations such as TAPOL and despite parliamentary opposition. The Indonesian military continued to use combat aircraft, helicopters, tanks, and a variety of weapons for military offensives in East Timor.

---

[50] Clwyd's communication with TAPOL representatives extended until at least the late 1990s, as evidenced by a letter in which "Paul" clarifies TAPOL's position on East Timor, which, he wrote, "has not changed." Letter to Ann Clwyd MP, July 14, 1998, *AMRT,* http://casacomum.org/cc/visualizador?pasta=06503.111.

[51] "Timor Oil Accord Sparks Row in Jakarta," *TAPOL Bulletin* 103, February 1991, 27.

[52] "Protest at BAe AGM Over Hawk Sales," *TAPOL Bulletin* 123, June 1984, 14.

[53] "Beating Swords into Ploughshares," *TAPOL Bulletin* 134, April 1996, 21.

[54] "Ploughshares Women Acquitted," *TAPOL Bulletin* 137, October 1996, 18–19.

[55] "The Falklands and East Timor," *TAPOL Bulletin* 51, May 1982, 4.

[56] "Halt the Offensive in East Timor! Impose an Arms Embargo on Indonesia!," *TAPOL Bulletin* 60, November 1983, 5.

Opening Up: A New Phase in the International Solidarity Movement

From the late 1980s, TAPOL reported increasing public opposition to the Suharto regime across Indonesia and in occupied East Timor, as well as the violent crackdowns that followed these actions. The most significant expression of popular discontent with the occupying regime, which was violently suppressed by Indonesian forces, was the Santa Cruz massacre in Dili on November 12, 1991. The front-page heading of the December 1991 bulletin read, "The killing fields of East Timor" and provided a report of the latest killings and massacres.[57] Due to the severity of the incident, the entire bulletin was devoted to East Timor. It was compiled very quickly, as news continued to flood in from inside the territory and around the world. The massacre marked a new phase in the international solidarity movement for East Timor. TAPOL's bulletin canvassed international outrage at the massacre, reproducing newspaper headlines and editorials of condemnation from around the world. Details of the massacre and the dramatic footage taken by British cameraman Max Stahl thrust East Timor onto television screens around the world, making it for the first time a major issue that Western powers could no longer afford to ignore.

Several other key developments were the focus of the international solidarity movement in the 1990s. The arrest and imprisonment of the resistance leader Xanana Gusmão on November 20, 1992, led to worldwide protests, calls for his release, and concern for his physical well-being. In a statement to the press just a few hours after his arrest, TAPOL called for his immediate and unconditional release and expressed concerns about his treatment in detention.[58] TAPOL also wrote to the UN Secretary-General, Boutros Boutros-Ghali, and the British government along the same lines.[59] From his cell in Cipinang prison in Jakarta, however, Gusmão continued to direct the resistance and to give interviews to journalists and human rights activists. For example, the Australian journalist John Pilger was able to make contact with Gusmão in 1995 through the clandestine network. Gusmão's interview with Pilger was published in newspapers around the world, including the December 1995 bulletin. The publication coincided with the twentieth anniversary of the Indonesian invasion and received far wider coverage than previous interviews with resistance leaders.[60] Further to these developments, the awarding of the 1996 Nobel Peace prize to Bishop Belo and José Ramos-Horta was, according to TAPOL, "a stunning victory for the people of East Timor and a humiliating defeat for the regime of President Suharto which has illegally occupied the country for twenty-one years."[61] These events further propelled the international movement for East Timor's independence into a new phase of activism.

Throughout the 1990s, TAPOL continued to follow developments on East Timor in the international sphere, including plans to send missions to East Timor to study the human rights situation there. From 1989, when the Indonesian government declared East Timor to be of "equal status" with the other Indonesian provinces, an increase in foreign

---

[57] "The Killing Fields of East Timor," *TAPOL Bulletin* 108, December 1991, 1.

[58] "Release Xanana Gusmao Immediately!," *TAPOL Bulletin* 114, December 1992, 18.

[59] "Release Xanana," 18.

[60] "Xanana Speaks to the World," *TAPOL Bulletin* 132, December 1995, 1–3.

[61] "Nobel Prize a Victory for East Timor," *TAPOL Bulletin* 138, December 1996, 1.

access to the territory led to more detailed reports of life under Indonesian rule.[62] Almost all of these reports attested to the prevalence of human rights abuses, the overwhelming presence of the Indonesian military, and the widespread atmosphere of fear. The UN Sub-Committee on the Prevention of Discrimination and Protection of Minorities also recognized the international situation and its conduciveness to dialogue, with Indonesia being increasingly "slammed" at the meetings and petitioners successively calling for East Timor's right to self-determination to be exercised.[63] Each year, TAPOL was among the many solidarity and human rights organizations from around the world that sent representatives to New York to petition the UN Special Committee on Decolonization on the "question of East Timor." Carmel Budiardjo attended the August 1991 meeting, for example, and her impressions and an assessment of the significance and limitations of the exercise were published in a subsequent bulletin.[64] Talks between Indonesia and Portugal continued to be held under the recommendation of the UN Secretary General, although TAPOL claimed that they "get nowhere" except to decide to hold another round of talks.[65]

TAPOL also engaged with the international solidarity movement throughout the 1990s, including participating in a series of seminars in Portugal that were organized by António Pinto Barbedo de Magalhães from Porto University and meetings organized by solidarity groups from across the globe. During this time, the international solidarity movement became extremely well-organized and coordinated; these developments contributed enormously to informing public opinion and forcing governments and institutions to acknowledge the injustice and brutality of Indonesia's occupation. TAPOL continued to report on the human rights situation as more massacres occurred in the 1990s, urging readers and supporters to write to key individuals to press for on-site UN monitoring, including Mary Robinson, UN Commissioner for Human Rights, the UK Foreign Secretary, and local MPs.[66] More than three hundred people attended a public meeting in 1995, at which John Pilger and Carmel Budiardjo spoke. TAPOL claimed that the size of the audience demonstrated a "steady rise in the number of people at public meetings about East Timor."[67]

Indonesian President Suharto's power began to wane in the late 1990s. In response, while maintaining a commitment to documenting developments in East Timor, TAPOL moved to pay more attention to the pro-democracy movement in Indonesia and to the economic crisis gripping the country. TAPOL profiled Indonesian advocates for East Timor's independence—or, at least, for an end to human rights violations being perpetrated—within the pro-democracy movement in Indonesia. When the end came for Suharto on May 21, 1998, TAPOL noted in its bulletin that among other human rights violations, Suharto had been "responsible for the deaths of 200,000 East Timorese, a third

---

[62] "The Future Management of East Timor," *TAPOL Bulletin* 91, February 1989, 14.

[63] "Indonesia Slammed at UN Decolonization Committee," *TAPOL Bulletin* 101, October 1990, 22.

[64] "East Timor at the UN Decolonization Committee," *TAPOL Bulletin* 107, October 1991, 13–16.

[65] "UN-Sponsored Tasks Get Nowhere," *TAPOL Bulletin* 115, February 1993, 8.

[66] "Human Rights Abuses Hit a New Low," *TAPOL Bulletin* 142, August 1997, 16.

[67] "CNRM Co-Chair Visits the UK," *TAPOL Bulletin* 128, April 1995, 8.

of the population, one of the worst acts of genocide this century."[68] The fall of Suharto marked the removal of a key obstacle to resolving the East Timor issue.

An announcement by the new Indonesian President B. J. Habibie in early 1999 symbolized the beginning of Indonesia's retreat from East Timor. However, from the onset, it was accompanied by a backlash of pro-integration paramilitary forces "spreading death and terror" across the territory, and TAPOL carefully tracked these developments.[69] Mass violence continued to sweep across East Timor throughout 1999 and particularly after the announcement that a popular consultation would be held on the issue of independence. TAPOL's statement to the UN Special Committee in 1999 attested to the atmosphere of "intimidation, threats and violence" present in East Timor that could undermine the integrity of the independence ballot.[70] Despite these circumstances, the people of East Timor voted overwhelmingly in favor of independence in the referendum on August 30, 1999.[71] The subsequent departure of the Indonesian military was accompanied by the destruction of much of East Timor's infrastructure and widespread killings. International organizations called desperately for an armed international force to be sent to the territory. Finally, upon the request of Indonesia, the UN Security Council adopted a resolution that led to the implementation of the International Force for East Timor (INTERFET), which began landing in Dili from September 20, 1999.[72] Finally, after a UN transitional period, on May 20, 2002, the Democratic Republic of Timor-Leste became a sovereign state.[73]

Independence and Issues of Redress

With the withdrawal of the Indonesian military in September 1999 and the country's move toward independence, TAPOL gradually reduced its focus on East Timor. After Indonesian troops left the territory, a new human rights situation emerged and the challenges of building a new state in the midst of widespread ruin became apparent. As such, TAPOL continued to track East Timor's transition to independent statehood, notably through firsthand visits to the territory. In December 1999 and January 2000, Liem Soei Liong traveled to East Timor for the first time and recorded his impressions of this new phase in East Timor's history.[74] Carmel Budiardjo similarly recorded her observations after visiting the territory for the first time in 2000.[75] In the bulletin, TAPOL continued to provide updates on challenges facing the new state, including the issue of East Timorese refugees trapped in camps in Indonesian West Timor, who had been forcibly evacuated following the referendum. With militia controlling the camps, it was extremely difficult for humanitarian agencies to provide relief and make arrangements

[68] "The End of Suharto," *TAPOL Bulletin* 147, July 1998, 1.

[69] "Indonesia's Retreat from East Timor," *TAPOL Bulletin* 151, March 1999, 1.

[70] "Statement on East Timor to the United Nations Special Committee, 23 June 1999," *TAPOL: Promoting Human Rights, Peace and Democracy in Indonesia*, http://tapol.org/news-and-reports/briefings/statement-east-timor-united-nations-special-committee-24-23-june-1999.

[71] "East Timor Wins its Independence," *TAPOL Bulletin* 154–55, November 1999, 5–10.

[72] "East Timor Wins," 5–10.

[73] UN Security Council, "Statement by the President of the Security Council," May 20, 2002, S/PRST/2002/13.

[74] "Impressions of East Timor," *TAPOL Bulletin* 157, April 2000, 8–11.

[75] "A Visit to the New East Timor, *TAPOL Bulletin* 161, March–April 2000, p. 8.

for repatriation. TAPOL followed the plight of these refugees who, it described, were "living in fear and confusion."[76] In August 2001, TAPOL wrote to the new Indonesian President Megawati Sukarnoputri to draw her attention to a number of issues that, it argued, had to be addressed to ensure that Indonesia's transition to democracy was based on respect for human rights and adherence to the rule of law. One of the three listed priority areas was West Timor. TAPOL representatives expressed concern that there was no apparent end to the crisis.[77]

Achieving national self-determination was just one goal of the international solidarity movement for East Timor. A new issue that arose was that of accountability and justice for the mass human rights violations that had been perpetrated by the Indonesian military and their auxiliaries. TAPOL traced the establishment of commissions investigating the violence in the lead-up to and following the referendum. In September 1999, the Indonesian government enacted a presidential decree in lieu of law for the formation of a human rights court; at the same time, the National Commission for Human Rights (KomnasHAM) set up a Commission to Investigate Violations of Human Rights to investigate abuses committed after the ballot. TAPOL repeatedly argued, however, that an international tribunal was the only way forward. Trials for crimes against humanity faced ongoing delays, ultimately resulting in "no justice" for East Timor, due to multiple acquittals and a series of unsatisfactory verdicts. TAPOL argued that this outcome only reinforced the view that Indonesia "is not committed to providing meaningful justice for the victims of human rights atrocities" in East Timor.[78] In January 2003, TAPOL participated in a symposium on Justice for International Crimes Committed in the Territory of East Timor, which was organized by the Asia Pacific Centre for Military Law of the University of Melbourne and the East Timorese NGO, Judicial System Monitoring Programme. At the symposium, participants agreed that the Jakarta trials were "a travesty of justice" and continued to push for an international justice mechanism.[79] These flaws were also identified by successive UN Special Rapporteurs that were sent to observe the processes. On October 20, 2004, TAPOL wrote to the newly inaugurated Indonesian president, Susilo Bambang Yudhoyono, proposing a human rights agenda for his new administration and calling for an end to impunity.[80] Finally in 2008, a New South Wales inquest into the deaths of the five journalists killed at Balibo in October 1975 handed down a ruling which contradicted Indonesia's insistence that the journalists had been killed in the crossfire. Instead, the inquest found that the killings were deliberate, the instructions had emanated from the highest echelons, and those responsible should be considered for possible war crimes prosecution.[81]

The other significant development in the independence era was the release of the final report of the CAVR, *Chega!*, which was set up as an independent body to inquire into human rights violations committed between 1974 and 1999. Notably, *Chega!* acknowledged TAPOL's role in "keeping the issue alive" in Britain through the

---

[76] 'East Timorese Refugees Still Stuck', *TAPOL Bulletin* 158, June 2000, p. 14.

[77] 'A Human Rights Agenda for Megawati', *TAPOL Bulletin* 163, October 2001, pp. 10–11.

[78] 'No Justice for East Timor', *TAPOL Bulletin* 169–70, January–February 2003, p. 20.

[79] 'No Justice', p. 21.

[80] 'A Human Rights Agenda for the New Government', *TAPOL Bulletin* 177, November 2004, pp. 4–5.

[81] 'Balibo Five Deliberately Killed, Says Coroner', *TAPOL Bulletin* 188–89, March 2008, p. 25.

publication of its newsletter, "whose regularity, longevity and professionalism was the envy of other activists."[82] Although TAPOL continued to express concern that the report was not being formally considered by the National Parliament of East Timor, it acknowledged the significant achievements of the commission in documenting the widespread and systematic violations of human rights that occurred throughout the Indonesian occupation. Most recently, after a decade-long advocacy effort by civil society and victim groups, an independent institution was established in East Timor in 2017 to facilitate the implementation of the recommendations of the CAVR report and the Indonesia–Timor-Leste Commission of Truth and Friendship: the National Chega! Centre (Centro Nasional Chega!, CNC).

Conclusion: A Weapon More Powerful than Guns

TAPOL was one of the key solidarity organizations involved in the international campaign that contributed to securing eventual self-determination for East Timor. Through its regular bulletin, TAPOL drew on a range of source material and collaborated with other organizations to provide regular updates on the human rights situation inside the territory. Most especially from 1979, when many other solidarity organizations fell by the wayside, TAPOL instead upped its campaign and continued to provide extensive coverage of the situation. One of the key platforms for action was the campaign for an arms embargo against Indonesia by the British government, and this issue attracted the attention and support of a range of organizations and prominent public figures.

TAPOL engaged a range of strategies in pursuing its aims: the regular *TAPOL Bulletin* was the most thorough and far-reaching, but TAPOL also produced pamphlets; organized demonstrations, speeches, and letter-writing campaigns; and testified at international commissions to raise awareness of the Indonesian occupation and to advocate fervently for national and international recognition. Significantly, TAPOL's campaigning did not cease when the East Timorese voted for independence in 1999: the organization continued to pay attention to the issues faced by the newly independent state. In particular, accountability for those responsible for mass human rights violations against the East Timorese people remained high on TAPOL's agenda, as it repeatedly called for an international tribunal as the only viable option to justice. As yet, these calls remain unheeded. However, TAPOL's contribution to the international solidarity movement for East Timor, "a weapon more powerful than guns,"[83] provides a distinct example of the possibilities of activist networks and global human rights activism in the Cold War era.

---

[82] CAVR, *Chega!*, p. 713.
[83] CAVR, *Chega!*, p. 713.

Solidarity for Solidarity: How the Indonesian Activists Gained Momentum for National Reformation (Reformasi) through Participating in the Transnational Solidarity Movement for East Timorese Self-Determination, 1995–99[1]

Pocut Hanifah

The struggle for democratic reform in Indonesia and the fight in East Timor have different agendas but the same enemy.[1]

Throughout most of the Indonesian occupation of East Timor, only a handful of Indonesian activists were concerned with the developments on this far-flung corner of

Pocut Hanifah has an MA in Southeast Asian Studies (Leiden), Junior Researcher on the project "The Self-determination of Timor-Leste: a study in Transnational History" (CES/UCoimbra)

[1] José Alexandre "Xanana" Gusmão, as paraphrased by the Indonesian activist Tri Agus S. Siswowihardjo. Tri Agus S. Siswowihardjo, "Reformasi dan Referendum Timtim," *Xpos* 38, no. 1 (September 19–25, 1998), 12. In Indonesian: "Perjuangan demokrasi di Indonesia dan perlawanan Timtim, mempunyai tujuan berbeda tetapi musuh yang sama." Xanana uttered this statement in his message during the Intra-East Timorese Dialogue (AETD) on April 27, 1998. See ft. 85. Xanana Gusmão, *To Resist Is to Win! The Autobiography of Xanana Gusmão* (Richmond, AUS: Aurora Books, 2000), 217.

the archipelago. The movement's involvement with the Timorese cause became more pronounced in the 1990s, but it is generally considered to have lagged behind in its response to the Santa Cruz Massacre of November 12, 1991, which evoked worldwide dismay at the Indonesian occupation of the former Portuguese colony. Nonetheless, as the Indonesian call for Timorese self-determination became more tangible halfway through the 1990s, so did the realization among East Timorese activists that both groups needed each other to achieve their aims.

Xanana's quote above reflects his conviction that "only in a Democratic Indonesia can the East Timorese conflict be resolved in a prompt matter."[2] This message was readily picked up by Indonesian activists who found themselves in the same prison block as Xanana in the hectic final years of the New Order regime (1995–98). This article discusses how halfway through the 1990s, the New Order's penitentiaries became the breeding ground of a Timorese-Indonesian solidarity movement that both sought democratic reform in Indonesia and self-determination of East Timor. The Indonesian and East Timorese activists had been driven behind the same bars by a shared enemy. While incarcerated together, they came to formulate a single agenda against "human right violations" that stretched beyond the predominantly local concerns that had characterized their earlier demonstrations.

Censored Solidarity under International Purview

Unlike other solidarity movements fighting for the same goals in democratic countries like Portugal, Australia, Japan, and the United States,[3] the Indonesian one spoke up while under the pressure of the same New Order regime that had invaded and occupied East Timor (1975–99). The fact that members of the Indonesian solidarity movement had to live under Suharto's repressive "New Order" regime (1966–98) limited their options to protest publicly for East Timor's right to self-determination. But despite being dangerous to talk about, the Indonesian occupation of East Timor was also full of potential to Indonesian activists who wished to underline the regime's suppression

---

[2] Translated from "hanya di negara Indonesia yang demokratislah masalah Timtim akan lebih cepat selesai." Siswowihardjo, "Reformasi dan Referendum," 12. On April 27, 1998, Gusmão addressed the Intra-East Timorese Dialogue (AETD, April 23–27, 1998)—which became the foundation of the East Timorese government: "Independence for East Timor will mean freedom for the Indonesian people. Justice and democracy in Indonesia will mean the liberation of the Maubere People." The full quote reads: "We also want to tell the Indonesian people that we closely follow the progress of the democracy movement in Indonesia. The Indonesian and Timorese peoples are fighting for different objectives which are based on the same principles of law, justice, freedom and peace. The two peoples—brothers, sisters and neighbours—are oppressed by the same repressive regime. Independence for East Timor will mean freedom for the Indonesian people. Justice and democracy in Indonesia will mean the liberation of the Maubere People." See also ft. 1. Gusmão, *To Resist*, 217.

[3] See Brad Simpson, "Solidarity in an Age of Globalization: The Transnational Movement for East Timor and US Foreign Policy," Peace & Change (2004): 453–82; Esther M. van den Berg, *The Influence of Domestic NGOs on Dutch Human Rights Policy: Case Studies on South Africa, Namibia, Indonesia and East Timor* (Antwerp: Intersentia-Hart, 2001), 217–360; Miguel Vale de Almeida, "Epilogue of Empire: East Timor and the Portuguese Postcolonial Catharsis," *Identities* 8, no. 4 (2001), 583–605. The archives of the American and Australian movement have been carefully archived by, respectively, the East Timor and Indonesia Action Network (ETAN, http://www.etan.org/etanpdf/timordocs/timordocs.htm) and the Clearing House for Archival Records on Timor (CHART, https://timorarchives.wordpress.com/category/about-blog/).

of ethnic minorities, farmers, workers, journalists, and students throughout the vast archipelago. After all, it was an issue that attracted much international attention.

For most Indonesian activists, East Timor represented all other Indonesian provinces that had suffered—and continued to suffer—under Suharto's militaristic regime. But unlike other provinces, East Timor—and the international conflict surrounding the 1989 Timor Gap Treaty between Indonesia and Australia—was always an international issue for the simple fact that Portugal was regarded by the United Nations as the legitimate administering power.[4] More so than the conflicts in Aceh, Papua, and the Moluccas, the occupation of East Timor was a diplomatic conundrum that involved many different parties across the globe.

The international concern for East Timor grew as the Cold War (1947–91) came to an end. The fall of the Berlin Wall in November 1989 opened new possibilities for the democratic opposition in Third World autocracies like Indonesia and revolutionized international politics. The strict anti-communist dictatorship of President Suharto was rendered swiftly redundant to the interests of Western powers. No longer would Jakarta be given a blank check to do what it liked in its illegally occupied "27th Province"— East Timor. [5] The widening international purview in the 1990s also increased pressure on Jakarta to engage in democratic reform. This benefitted East Timorese as well as Indonesian activists, whose demonstrations, arrests, and imprisonment were reported on by well-known humanitarian organizations.

In newspapers like the Australian socialist *Green Left* weekly, the Indonesian activists incarcerated by the New Order regime were portrayed as martyrs fighting for "human rights" in Java, Sumatra, as well as East Timor. It is in this context that Indonesian penitentiaries became a source of resistance. Behind bars, Indonesian activists came to adopt the jargon of human rights groups to advocate their own interests. For many among them, advocating East Timorese self-determination was one of the more potent ways to gather international solidarity for their own struggle for democratic reform in Indonesia.[6] The political prisoners from East Timor with whom they shared their prison blocks often became close acquittances or even friends. This article will discuss how this "comradeship" influenced the agenda of parts of the Indonesian protest movement in the years preceding the national reformation of Indonesia in 1998.

---

[4] Lisbon never ceded this right of sovereignty despite immense pressure from Indonesia and its Western allies in the mid- to late 1970s following Indonesia's invasion of December 6–7, 1975. The East Timor "issue" thus remained on the books of the UN Security Council and General Assembly throughout the twenty-four years of the Indonesian military occupation from December 1975 to September 1999. Eventually, following the August 30, 1999 popular referendum when 78.5 percent of East Timorese voters chose the independence option, the combined pressure of the United States and the will of the international community through the UN Security Council's Chapter VII decision of September 15, 1999 (SCR 1264) sanctioned a multinational force to protect the United Nations Mission in East Timor (UNAMET) forced Indonesia's military withdrawal.

[5] Amitav Acharya, "Developing Countries and the Emerging World Order Security and Institutions," in *The Third World Beyond the Cold War: Continuity and Change*, ed. Louise Fawcett and Yezid Sayigh (Oxford: Oxford University Press, 2003), 81–83.

[6] For a discussion on the notions of human dignity and modernity—both of European origin, but since then contextualized in societies across the world—that gave birth to the notion of human rights, see Amos Nascimento and Matthias Lutz-Bachmann, "Human Dignity in the perspective of a Critical Theory of Human Rights," in *Human Dignity: Perspectives from a Critical Theory of Human Rights*, ed. Amos Nascimento and Matthias Lutz-Bachmann (New York: Routledge, 2018), 20–23.

Simultaneously, I will also argue that "solidarity" was a tactically refined diplomatic decision made to find a way out of the corner to which the Indonesian activists had been driven by Suharto's regime. In this sense, their solidarity toward East Timor was a means to break through dichotomies that had been propagated by the New Order along the lines of its subjects either being Indonesian/East Timorese, Nationalist/Communist, and Javanese/primitive. Through alliances with their East Timorese peers in prison, the Indonesian activists discussed in this article succeeded in harnessing the support of foreign diplomats and solidarity movements in defiance of reified narratives that had been carefully produced by the New Order regime between 1975 and 1995 to legitimize the "integration" of East Timor to their Indonesian citizens.

At the same time, the Indonesian activists also reproduced several underlying biases in the Western-centric human rights advocacy that tended to simplify the role of the Indonesian regime in the conflict and turn all who were part of the Indonesian state and its armed forces—even foot soldiers—into villainous human right violators without studying their motives carefully. The adaptation of the human rights discourse was never straightforward, however, and Indonesian activists did add their own layers of sophistication to translate and contextualize concepts that were originally based on a fundamentally Western understanding of the world.

This article will reflect on whether the Indonesian activism for East Timorese self-determination can be considered as a form of anticolonial solidarity that sought to overcome the abyssal genealogy of the conventional human rights discourse. As has recently been emphasized by the ALICE research project, the original hegemonic concept of human rights divided the world into the Global South and North and only cared to acknowledge rights of individuals activists and states, not communities within provinces of "third world" countries. Taking this in mind, I will consider to what extent the Indonesian solidarity movement reiterated Portuguese, British, Dutch, and Australian beliefs of what decolonization and globalization was meant to entail.[7]

The Indonesian activists discussed in this paper were all aware that their main struggle was to convince Indonesian peasants and workers to join their movement and oppose the neoliberal exploitation of communities and natural resources in places like East Timor, but also Java. To further this aim, they needed the attention and support of the Western solidarity movements too, especially when they themselves became targeted by the New Order regime. They subsequently, reconfigured their narratives in support of the diplomatic turn taken by the Habibie government in 1998–99. The interaction of the Indonesian activists with these two very different audiences and the way in which solidarity obtained for one cause was reutilized *and* recontextualized for another proves to be an interesting example of how intercultural translation can lead to a reconstruction of what human rights and the related notion of democratization entails when fought for in a fully transnational solidarity network.

---

[7] Nelson Maldonado-Torres, "On the Coloniality of Human Rights," *Revista Crítica de Ciências Sociais* 114 (2017): 118–25, 128–32; Boaventura de Sousa Santos and Bruno Sena Martins, "Introduction," in *The Pluriverse of Human Rights: The Diversity of Struggles for Dignity*, ed. Boaventura de Sousa Santos and Bruno Sena Martins (New York: Routledge, 2021), 1–16; Boaventura de Sousa Santos, "Human Right, Democracy and Development," in de Sousa Santos and Martins, *The Pluriverse of Human Rights*, 21–36; George N. Fourlas, *Anti-Colonial Solidarity: Race, Reconciliation, and MENA Liberation* (London: Rowman & Littlefield, 2022), 1–17.

Senior Indonesian activists

Other than the paper written by the well-known Indonesian intellectual and activist George Junus Aditjondro (1946–2016) during his exile in Australia in the late 1990s, the Indonesian solidarity movement has to date received limited coverage.[8] The solidarity movement *within* Indonesia has been discussed, but mainly from the perspective of the East Timorese students and foreign activists.[9] These East Timorese and foreign—often Australian—activists closely interacted with their Indonesian peers. Both the Indonesian and East Timorese transnational networks spread far abroad and linked these movements closely with the solidarity movements in the countries of the two former colonizers of Indonesia and East Timor: the Netherlands and Portugal.

Transnational networks were fundamental to the internal coherence of the Indonesian solidarity movement. At the same time, the public participation of Indonesian activists in the Timorese, Portuguese, Australian, and Dutch solidarity movements legitimized their cause for democratic reform by connecting the Indonesian occupation of East Timor with the more wide-scale abuse of human rights and suppression of political freedoms that Indonesians were experiencing under Suharto's New Order. The egregious atrocities committed by the Indonesian military in East Timor symbolized the worst human rights abuses of the New Order, whose power was as contested by popular activist groups inside Indonesia as it was by the East Timorese independence movement outside the Republic in their illegally occupied territory. It is important to note that Indonesian activists at large only began to adopt this "anti-Suharto, pro-East Timor" narrative a few years before Suharto's May 21, 1998 downfall. But they did do so at a crucial turning point of which the significance can only be fully understood by reviewing the emergence of a new generation of Indonesian protestors in the early 1990s.

Originally, support for East Timor's struggle for independence in Indonesia came from a handful of politically engaged NGOs like the Institute for Policy Research and Advocacy (ELSAM) and the Indonesian Human Rights Institute (LPHAM).[10] The latter was headed up by the Dutch deserter turned lawyer, Haji Johannes Cornelius (Poncke) Princen, who had been given Indonesian citizenship in 1949 and was considered as a modern-day Multatuli—an advocate for the colonized—by several Indonesian

[8] George J. Aditjondro, *Challenges and Prospects of the Indonesian Pro-East Timor Movement* (New South Wales: Newcastle University, 1997); which was translated into Indonesian in *Menyongsong Matahari Terbit di Puncak Ramelau: Dampak Pendudukan Timor Lorosa'e dan Munculnya Gerakan pro-Timor Lorosa'e di Indonesia* (Jakarta: Yayasan Hak dan Fortilos, 2000), 249–61. It does not occur in the English version of this book, which was published three years earlier in Australia. See also George J. Aditjondro, *Timor Lorosa'e on the Crossroad: Timor Lorosa'e's Transformation from Jakarta's Colony to a Global Capitalist Outpost* (Jakarta: Center for Democracy and Social Justice Studies, 2001), 138. For Timorese activists who grew up under the Indonesian regime, see Peter Carey, "Third-World Colonialism, the Geração Foun, and the Birth of a New Nation: Indonesia through East Timorese Eyes, 1975–99," *Indonesia* 76 (2003): 23–67; Angie Bexley, "The Geracao Foun, Talitakum and Indonesia: Media and Memory Politics in Timor Leste," *Review of Indonesian and Malaysian Affairs* 4, no. 1 (2007): 71–90; Angie Bexley and Nuno Rodrigues Tchailoro, "Consuming Youth: Timorese in the Resistance Against Indonesian Occupation," *The Asia Pacific Journal of Anthropology* 14, no. 5 (2013): 405–22; Takahiro Kamisuna, "Beyond Nationalism: Youth Struggle for the Independence of East Timor and Democracy for Indonesia," *Indonesia* 110 (2020): 82–85.

[9] Kirsty Sword Gusmão, *A Woman of Independence* (Sydney: Macmillan Australia, 2007); Carey, "Third-World Colonialism."

[10] ELSAM stands for Lembaga Studi Advokasi Masyarakat, LPHAM for Lembaga Pembela Hak-Hak Azasi Manusia.

activists.[11] His NGO had delivered reports of torture, abductions, and other atrocities that Princen with great bravery had been alerting international parties to since 1966.[12] Poncke's private letters describe how senior Portuguese government officials called him in the middle of the night to ask about Bishop Belo's health condition. He also handed memoranda on East Timor to the US Vice President Dan Quayle during the latter's state visit to Indonesia in 1989 and tried to reach out to Pope John Paul II a few months after. In June 1993, he met Portugal's President Mário Soares when the latter tried to handle the appeal for political asylum by seven young East Timorese who had entered the Swedish and Finnish embassies in Jakarta.[13] Poncke housed ex-Fretilin members and Portuguese Jesuits and was closely involved with Indonesian activists, yet he did not have a mass movement backing him and mostly relied on international diplomatic networks to make an impact on Suharto's regime.[14]

The links between these Indonesian NGOs and Europe were thick. Dutch and English organizations like TAPOL (1973–2008), Komitee Indonesië (The Indonesian Committee, 1968–97),[15] and Radio Nederland (RANESI) had also a long track record of distributing reports on human right violations in East Timor. These were compiled by prominent Indonesian human rights activists and political commentators like the TAPOL founder Carmel Budiardjo, the TAPOL member Liem S. Liong (1943), and RANESI radio journalist Aboeprijadi Santoso (Tossi) (1947).[16]

---

[11] These NGOs later formed the Joint Committee for East Timor, see Robinson, *If You Leave Us Here*, 85. Naldo Rei, *Resistance: A Childhood Fighting for East Timor* (St. Lucia, AUS: University of Queensland Press, 2007), 205–6; Comissão para os Direitos do Povo Maubere, A Indonésia na Região Ásia-Pacífico (Lisbon: CDPM, 1994), 35; H. J. C. Princen, *70 Tahun; Gerilya Yang Tak Pernah Selesai* (Jakarta: Panitia 70 Tahun H. J. C. Princen, 1995); Arjan Onderdenwijngaard, *Multatuli Leeft in Lebak: Honderdzestig jaar Max Havelaar in Indonesië* (Amsterdam: De Geus, 2021), 30–31; Wilson, "Poncke Princen adalah Multatuli, Sneevliet dan Douwes Dekker," *Sinar Harapan* (March 2, 2002); Asvi Warman Adam, "Tokoh Langka H. Poncke Princen," *Superhalaman*, March 14, 2007, https://superhalaman.wordpress.com/2007/03/14/ibrahim-isa-tokoh-langka-h-poncke-princen.

[12] Pat Walsh, *Arrests and Detentions of East Timorese students in Bali* (Fitzroy: ACFOA, 1990), 1; Haji Johannes Cornelius (Ponke) Princen, *Prime Minister of Japan, Mr. Toshiki Kaifu* (Jakarta: Institute for the Defence of Human Rights in Indonesia, 1990), 1–2; Haji Johannes Cornelius (Ponke) Princen and Carmel Budiardjo, *Daftar namanama rakyat Timor Timur yong dibunuh tahun 1989* (London: Tapol, 1989), 2; Diane Orentlicher, *Human Rights in Indonesia and East Timor* (New York: Asia Watch Committee, 1989), 122, 147, 158.

[13] Amnesty International, *Indonesia / East Timor: Seven East Timorese still in Danger* (New York: Amnesty International, 1993), 1–13; Aditjondro, *Challenges and Prospects*, 1–2.

[14] The Adjoint Minister to the Prime Minister of Portugal Mário Soares, António de Almeida Santos, is specifically mentioned by Poncke. Poncke Princen, "Letter to His Son Iwan and His Daughter Joke," Jakarta, September 10, 1989; Poncke Princen, "Letter to His Son Nico," Jakarta, November 14, 1989; Poncke Princen, "Letter to His Son Nico," Jakarta, February 10, 1990; Poncke Princen, "Letter to His Former Partner Els," Jakarta, May 20, 1990. International Institute of Social History (from now on abbreviated to ISSG), ARCH02152.

[15] "Tapol Bulletin," Research Repository Victoria University, accessed February 8, 2022, http://vuir.vu.edu.au/cgi/search/archive/simple?order=date/creators_name/title&_action_search=Reorder&screen=Search&dataset=archive&exp=0|1|-date/creators_name/title|archive|-|q:abstract/creators_name/date/documents/title:ALL:IN:tapol+bulletin|-|eprint_status:eprint_status:ANY:EQ:archive|metadata_visibility:metadata_visibility:ANY:EQ:show; "Komitee Indonesië en Stichting Informatie Indonesië," ISSG, ARCH01623, 200–4.

[16] The interview was conducted on February 12, 2020 in his house in central Amsterdam. Tapol is an acronym for political prisoners or *Tahanan Politik* in Indonesian. The interview was conducted on January 20, 2020 in his house in central Amsterdam. Aboeprijadi Santoso, *Jejak-jejak darah: tragedi & pengkhianatan di Timor Timur* (Amsterdam: INHAM, 1996); Carmel Budiardjo and Liem Soei Liong, *The War against East Timor* (London: Zed, 1984); Carmel Budiardjo, *Surviving Indonesia's Gulag: A Western Woman Tells Her Story* (London: Cassell, 1996).

The Indonesian mass killings of 1965–66, which established the New Order regime, galvanized these groups into being. The Komitee Indonesië was founded in 1968 by the Dutch Marxist sociologist Willem Frederik Wertheim (1907–98) to investigate the reports of the 1965–66 killings on Java. His organization soon came to attract Indonesian refugees who had lost their passport due to being classified as Communists. On their turn, these refugees extended the focus of the Komitee to occupied territories like West Papua and East Timor. The Indonesian activist A. Umar Said (1926–2011), for instance, advocated the cause of East Timor to Wertheim when frequenting the Netherlands between 1976 and 1982. He ended up cofounding the Paris-based Commission of Solidarity for East Timor (Komite Solidaritas Timor Timur) in 1976, which itself became the bedrock for the French branch of TAPOL that was established two years later.[17] Due to its connections with other killings and human right violations, these activists were already deeply involved with East Timor long before the Santa Cruz Massacre.[18] But their message never resounded strongly in Indonesia itself.

The international influence of the first generation of Indonesian activists, and their often-costly personal sacrifices, underscore that they had engaged in political activism for decades; TAPOL (1973) predating the Indonesian invasion of East Timor in December 1975 by a full two years. Moreover, they were all reliant on contributions from members of the worldwide solidarity network and thus had to ensure the engagement of their international sponsors and audience. Their dependence on funding from Western sponsors and their non-Indonesian origin, in the case of Princen and Budiardjo, made it easier for the Indonesian regime to dismiss their activism as a tool of foreign interests. The ageing Princen, in particular, was regularly harassed, being called into Indonesian military headquarters in the post-Santa Cruz Massacre period to undergo repeated interrogations for a variety of demonstrations, most of which did not relate to his organization, LPHAM. Still, his popular appeal was only marginal compared to that which he had enjoyed in the early 1950s when his contributions as an Indonesian guerrilla fighter during the Independence War (1945–49) were still fresh in the memory of the postwar Republican political elite. The intimidation of this septuagenarian Dutch-born human rights supporter simply did not raise the same kind of international rejection as the imprisonment of Indonesian and Timorese activists.[19]

New Wave of Protests in the Early 1990s

The younger generation of Indonesian student and union activists was a more pressing concern for Suharto than LPHAM or TAPOL. The Indonesian pro-democracy and labor union movements both represented important sections of Indonesian society that had become alienated from his regime. In particular, as the Indonesian middle class had grown in size and affluence, so their better educated offspring, along Muchtar Pakpahan's first independent trade union, SBSI (Indonesian Workers Welfare Union), began to demand

[17] A. Umar Said, *Perjalan Hidup Saya* (Jakarta: Yayasan Pancur Siwah, 2004), xvi, 148-49, 155, 185, 195, 252, 280, 296, 298. Interview with Aboeprijadi Santoso in Amsterdam on November 14, 2021.

[18] Only ELSAM could be said to have switched its focus as a consequence of the 1991 bloodbath. Janet E. Hunt, "Local NGOs in National Development: The Case of East Timor" (PhD diss., Royal Melbourne Institute of Technology, 2008), 154–55, 233–34.

[19] Comissão para os Direitos do Povo Maubere, *A Indonésia na Região Ásia-Pacífico* (Lisbon: CDPM, 1994), 35; Joyce van Fenema and Poncke Princen, *Een Kwestie van Kiezen* (Den Haag: BZZTôH, 1995).

greater freedoms of association and wage bargaining. The pro-democracy groups and labor unions increasingly resented the intrusions of the Indonesian army and police in their work places and daily lives.[20]

Between 1993 and 1996, mass protests in Jakarta started to resemble the 1974 Malari incident—which were the first to fully expose and publicly criticize the corruption of the New Order oligarchy—and predictably led to bans of critical newspapers and an increase in civil intelligence operations similar to what had happened twenty years earlier. Admittingly, the first major protest was led by blue-collar metalheads in April 1993 who had little to no concern for what happened in East Timor.[21] But most of the protests in the subsequent two years were orchestrated by students and journalists who did see ways to tie the anger of marginalized workers to that felt by the many victims of Indonesia's military operations. Muchtar Pakpahan was one of the first to explicitly denounce the Indonesian occupation of East Timor but dropped the subject after his statements on East Timor were used by the government to classify his union strikes as attempts to "overthrow, damage or undermine state power." After a short prison sentence, he reserved the topic for international conferences rather than rallies in Indonesia where the security forces kept their eyes on him.[22]

Similarly, Siswa Santoso—a Javanese activist of the National Farmers' Union (STN)—appropriated the call for East Timorese self-determination to highlight his own concerns about mass expropriation of rural landholdings by New Order regime cronies. In a letter sent to the United Nations' Commission on Human Rights (UNHCR) in March 1993, Santoso detailed the torture endured by Javanese farmers protesting an Indonesian army land-grab only to conclude with a call for "concrete action to investigate the human rights situation in Indonesia and in the occupied territories of Aceh and East Timor."[23] He had bundled his letter in with the petition of an East Timorese women's rights activist thus joining the two concerns in a single agenda item.[24] At a stroke, Javanese farmers and Timorese rebels were now one and the same—not Communists but both victims of Suharto's New Order. Like Pakpahan, however, Santoso needed to be careful when tying these issues together on Indonesian soil, as the New Order regime was quick to react to such joined calls for action and STN risked compromising its political support for Javanese farmers by Santoso's open support for East Timorese self-determination.

[20] SBSI stands for Serikat Buruh Seluruh Indonesia. E. Aspinall, *Opposing Suharto: Compromise, Resistance, and Regime Change in Indonesia* (Stanford: Stanford University Press, 2005), 130–31; Aditjondro, Challenges and Prospects, 6–8.

[21] These fans had gathered to attend a concert by the American metal band Metallica. The high demand for tickets led to exorbitant prices and forced a large group of youngsters to listen to the echoes of guitar riffs and double bass drums from outside the stadium. Feeling belittled and angry at once, the protesters set alight parts of the surrounding elite Lebak Bulus neighborhood. Emma Baulch, "Alternative Music and Mediation in Late New Order Indonesia," *Inter-Asia Cultural Studies* 3, no. 2 (2002): 219, 227–29.

[22] Mochtar Pakpahan, *Untukmu buruh penjara kutempuh: sebuah catatan harian di penjara*, vol. 1 (Jakarta: Pustaka Forum Adil Sejahtera,1996); Amnesty International, *Indonesia: The trial of thought* (March 31, 1997), Index Number: ASA 21/019/1997, 13; Adi Andojo Soetjipto, "Legal Reform and Challenges in Indonesia," in *Indonesia in Transition: Social Aspects of Reformasi and Crisis*, ed. Chris Manning and Peter van Diermen (London: Zed Books, 2000), 271; Aditjondro, *Challenges and Prospects*, 7–8.

[23] Siswa Santoso and Alexandra Reis, *Statement by Alexandra Reis and Siswa Santoso: Commission on Human Rights, 49th session Agenda Item 12* (Geneva: United Nations, 1993), 3.

[24] Santoso and Reis, *Statement*, 1–5.

In 1994–95, the Indonesian solidarity movement for East Timor was picked up by a younger group of Indonesian activists who enjoyed much smaller constituencies than established union leaders like Pakpahan. This also entails that they had less to lose. The movement was principally represented by the People's Democratic Association/Party (PRD) under the leadership of Budiman Sudjatmiko—an alumnus of Yogyakarta's Gadjah Mada University—and its general secretary, Petrus Hariyanto.[25] Officially founded on May 23, 1994, the PRD was to all intents and purposes a continuation of the Yogyakarta Students Solidarity (SMY) movement that had been active since the late 1980s. Still, its field of political interest had broadened compared to the early days of SMY. The PRD board member and cofounder Dita Indah Sari had been particularly active in reaching out to laborers across Java, thereby broadening their backing from campus to kampong.[26] Student members remained the party's main component and gathered under the banner of SMID—the Students in Solidarity with Democracy in Indonesia, founded in 1994.[27] But PRD was supported by a broader section of society through its associations with the Peoples' Artists Network (JAKER) and two influential labour unions: the National Farmers' Union (STN) and Indonesian Workers' Struggle Center (PPBI).[28]

The PRD was banned in July 1996 as a result of their unwavering political backing of the opposition leader Megawati Sukarnoputri—who had recently been ousted as head of the Indonesian Democratic Party (PDI) through pressure from the government—and honors bestowed on Xanana and the author Pramoedya Ananta Toer.[29] The frictions between PRD and the Indonesian regime escalated on July 27, 1996, when Indonesian government forces took hold of the head office of the Indonesian Democratic Party to evict the supporters of Megawati who refused to leave the office building after their patron's forced removal as leader of their party.[30] In need of a scapegoat, the government

---

[25] PRD stands for Persatuan/Partai Rakyat Demokratik.

[26] Dita Indah Sari, *Dn. Aidit Terbahak-Bahak Dari Liang Kuburnya: Pembelaan dalam perkara para terdakwa 1. Dita Indah Sari 2. Coen Husein Pontoh* (Surabaya: Tim Pembela Hukum & Keadilan Indonesia, 1997); Wilson bin Nurtyas, "Dita Indah Sari [24 th], Indonesia: Dia Berdemonstrasi Menuntut Upah Minimum Yang Iebih Tinggi" [translation of "Zij demonstreerde voor een hoger minimumloon," Wimanjaya, trans.], in ISSG, ARCH02712_2005.

[27] SMID stands for Solidaritas Mahasiswa Indonesia untuk Demokrasi. The PRD was renamed to Partai Rakyat Demokratik (People's Democratic Party) in 1996, see Aspinall, *Opposing Suharto*, 130, 296.

[28] JAKER stands for *Jaringan Kesenian Rakyat* / The cooperation between JAKER and PRD led to internal discord among JAKER's members: Javanese painters, sculptors, poets and musicians who sought to emphasize JAKER artistic ambitions that could be threatened by political interference. Arif Zulkifli, Seno Joko Suyono, and Purwanto Setiadi, *Prahara Orde Baru Wiji Thukul* (Jakarta: Gramedia, 2013), 65, 67, 115–16, 127. STN stands for Serikat Tani Nasional, PPBI for Pusat Perjuangan Buruh Indonesia. Geoff Simons, *Indonesia: The Long Oppression* (Houndmills, Basingstoke: Macmillan Press, 2000), 9–10; Wilson bin Nurtyas, *The Indonesian Pro-Democracy Movement and Maubere Peoples' Independence: Position Paper Prepared by Solidaritas Perjuangan Rakyat Indonesia dengan Maubere and SPRIM—Indonesian Peoples Solidarity Struggle with the Maubere People* (Lisbon: SPRIM, 1996), 21–22. Note that Wilson bin Nurtyas's curriculum vitae mentions him as the author of the SPRIM booklet mentioned above, Wilson bin Nurtyas, *Curriculum Vitae* (2003), 2, in ISSG, ARCH02712.ACCRUAL2012.

[29] Sudjatmiko was arrested on August 4, 1996 (he served two-and-a-half years of a thirteen-year jail sentence only being released on December 10, 1999 a full nineteen months after Suharto's fall). Aspinall, *Opposing Suharto*, 124, 130–44, 167–68, 181, 186–89, 192–97, 201, 212–14, 225, 227–28, 255, 260, 266, 282, 285–88.

[30] D. Ziv, "Populist Perceptions and Perceptions of Populism in Indonesia: The Case of Megawati Soekarnoputri," *South East Asia Research* 9, no. 1 (2001): 76, 79; Stefan Eklöf Amirell, *Power and Political Culture in Suharto's Indonesia: The Indonesian Democratic Party (PDI) and the Decline of the New Order (1986–98)* (London: Routledge, 2004), 263–76.

targeted PRD after these actions occurred. Still, the government failed to stop the movement.

After the ban, PRD remained politically active and would play an important role in Suharto's downfall. The suppression of the party by the New Order regime backfired as the PRD as well as its political agenda gained a degree of popularity within Indonesia when their members used their trials as a means to advocate their party line in public. The general sympathy expressed for these "dissidents" became more noticeable as the Asian Financial Crisis pulled more and more Indonesians under the poverty line between 1997 and 1998.[31] Unlike LPHAM or TAPOL, PRD managed to reach out to the masses by making them aware of their actions and struggles against the regime. In their flyers, some PRD activists claimed that their more radical provincial and campus-based branches could attract ten thousand peasants and about ten thousand to fifteen thousand workers thanks to their alliances with STN and PPBI.[32]

Through rallies, websites, news articles, and pamphlets, PRD's leaders created a general sense of shared suffering with Suharto's "political captives" among their Indonesian followers. These victims included the stigmatized "Communist" detainees who had been arrested in the bloody events following the September 30/October 1, 1965 "coup" that brought Suharto to power, but also the recently captured Xanana. For some of the Indonesian activists—whether in or outside of PRD—East Timor would even become the focus of campaigns for political change in Indonesia. These noticeably included the students Wilson bin Nurtyas and Yenny Rosa Damayanti and also journalist Tri Agus Susanto Siswowiharjo, whose actions, affiliations, and imprisonment I will return to in the following pages.[33]

The support for self-determination for East Timor was mentioned during the founding congress of the PRD in 1994 and had been publicly advocated by PRD board members during a forum in Sydney on December 2, 1994, but it would only become a major theme for the party a year later.[34] Wilson explicitly acknowledges that Poncke Princen—who he refers to as a mentor and even "grandfather"—inspired him to focus on East Timor in 1995.[35] At the same time, the general engagement of Indonesian youth was also encouraged by Xanana himself, who had been calling for Indonesian solidarity in the months after his arrest. From his cell, this central figure of the East Timorese resistance movement actively steered East Timorese students on Java to approach Indonesian activists to breathe new life into their campaign. This took time to happen but eventually succeeded.

[31] A. Suryahadi, S. Sumarto, and L.Pritchett, "Evolution of Poverty during the Crisis in Indonesia," *Asian Economic Journal* 17, no. 3 (2003): 221–41; Riyana Miranti, "Poverty in Indonesia 1984–2002: The Impact of Growth and Changes in Inequality," *Bulletin of Indonesian Economic Studies* 46, no. 1 (2010): 82–83, 86.

[32] Kees van Dijk, *A Country in Despair: Indonesia between 1997 and 2000* (Leiden: KITLV, 2001), 17, 21–22, 30, 42, 92, 127–28, 132, 171–73, 215, 225, 236, 332–33, 435, 454, 464; Wilson, *The Indonesian Pro-Democracy Movement*, 1–18, 22–23. This claim is made on page 9 and 18.

[33] Note that "bin Nurtyas" is not a surname but simply a reference to Wilson's father.

[34] Max Lane, "Indonesian Solidarity with the Struggle for Timor-Leste's Independence in the 1990s," in *Timor-Leste 1999: 20 Years On*, ed. Steven Farram, Dulce Martins da Silva , Leonardo F. Soares, Nuno Canas Mendes, Clinton Fernandes, Mica Barreto Soares, Uka Pinto, Hannah Loney, Robert L Williams, Claudino Ninas Nabais, and Michael Leach, 22–23.

[35] Adam, "Tokoh Langka."

RENETIL

The Indonesian solidarity movement for East Timor gained momentum when a young generation of Timorese activists reached out to their Indonesian peers. In the wake of his capture in November 1992, the central leader of the Timorese Independence movement, Xanana Gusmão, ordered the Timorese students of the National Resistance of East Timorese Students (RENETIL, founded in Denpasar, Bali, on June 20, 1988) to involve Indonesian sympathizers in their movement.[36] Indonesian student activists, farmers, and journalists were particularly targeted. By late 1994, RENETIL, operating out of its principal bases in Denpasar, Yogyakarta, and Jakarta, had succeeded in drawing close ties to the Indonesian democratic reform movement.

From its very foundation, RENETIL's principal goal was to draw international attention to the East Timorese struggle. The November 12, 1991 Santa Cruz massacre was a turning point here.[37] The international outrage in the wake of the massacre—which took the life of 271 East Timorese and led to an equal number of missing persons—made RENETIL aware that in the post-Cold War era, human rights issues were now central to international relations.[38] The greater international scrutiny of Indonesia's human rights record in East Timor and elsewhere enhanced East Timor's diplomatic effort.[39]

The long years of José Ramos-Horta's lonely struggle at the UN and elsewhere in the 1980s—particularly in Portugal itself and its former African colonies of Guinea-Bissau, Angola, and Mozambique—were now superseded by an invigorated multi-lateral diplomacy spearheaded by the likes of Portugal's President, Mário Soares, within the European Union and other international fora. This in turn helped to increase global interest in East Timor's political fate, which now became a concern of international diplomacy and also raised the former Portuguese colony's profile at the UN as well as solidarity movements around the world. In the post-Cold War era this would prove crucial to securing East Timor's independence vote in August 1999 and the subsequent UN Chapter VII-mandated intervention.

In this context, the Timorese student members of RENETIL also learned that their diplomatic stand would benefit greatly from closer association with sympathetic Indonesian student organizations as part of their larger strategy of "Indonesianizing" the East Timor conflict (Indonesiação do Conflito de Timor-Leste).[40] As such, East Timorese and Indonesian activists were able to highlight the true nature of Suharto's New Order— no longer a moderately successful neoliberal developmentalist regime, but a systematic

---

[36] RENETIL stands for Resistência Nacional dos Estudantes de Timor-Leste. Michael Leach, *Nation-Building and National Identity in Timor-Leste* (New York: Routledge, 2017), 85, 101–11, 117–19; Kelly Silva, "Reciprocity, Recognition and Suffering. Political Mobilizers in Independent East Timor," *Vibrant Virtual Brazilian Anthropology* (VIBRANT) 5, no. 2 (2008), 156–78; G. Robinson, *If You Leave Us Here, We Will Die: How Genocide Was Stopped in East Timor* (Princeton: Princeton University Press, 2011), 81–82. Interview with Yenny Rosa Damayanti, June 25, 2020, via WhatsApp; G. J. Aditjondro, "Prospek pembangunan Timor Timur, sesudah penangkapan Xanana Gusmao," *Hayam Wuruk* 8, no. 3 (1993), 62–67.

[37] IMPETTU stands for Ikatan Mahasiswa dan Pelajar Timor Timur.

[38] "ETAN Backgrounder: Santa Cruz Massacre," East Timor and Indonesia Action Network, accessed March 4, 2023, http://www.etan.org/factsheets/santa_cruz.htm; Amy Rothschild, "Human Rights in Timor-Leste's Struggle for Independence," *Indonesia* 115 (2023): 19–20.

[39] Robinson, *If You Leave Us Here*, 66–91.

[40] Takahiro, "Beyond Nationalism," 77, 82; Rei, *Resistance*, 205–6.

human rights violator.[41] The cooperation between the East Timorese and Indonesian activists—and also the Indonesian solidarity movement that stemmed from this—did, however, only take concrete form in 1994, three years after the Santa Cruz Massacre and two years after Xanana's call for further engagement between the two. This seemingly slow response to the unfolding tragedies in East Timor underlines the complex dilemmas that Indonesian activists faced when criticizing their own suppressive government.

Indonesian Weeklies

Although some Indonesian students had signed petitions and joined demonstrations directly after the Santa Cruz Massacre, the first organized efforts to address East Timor in Indonesia were made by critical journalists though the Information Centre and Action Network for Reform (PIJAR), Institute for the Research of People's Rights (LEKHAT), and Indonesian Front for the Defence of Human Rights (INFIGHT).[42] INFIGHT had participated in the demonstration in front of the United Nations representative office in Jakarta on November 19, 1991, but the subsequent crackdown by the Indonesia police prevented the organization from reaching out to a larger Indonesian audience. These three organizations only obtained significant following in the second half of the year 1994 in the wake of the effective banning of the mainstream *Tempo*, *DeTik*, and *Editor* weeklies on June 21, 1994.[43] By stopping the mass circulations of these progressive magazines,

---

[41] These Indonesian activists actively contested the New Order regime's historiography, which claimed that Jakarta had liberated East Timor from its Portuguese and Communist oppressors in 1975. Indonesian school children were taught—and appropriate curricula developed—that Indonesia had "fought for East Timor" in the name of "supporting freedom from Portuguese colonialism," a "noble struggle" in line with the decolonization goals set out in the April 1955 Asia Africa Conference (KAA) hosted by Indonesia. Note that the New Order curriculum often used publications of local customs (*adat*) and folklore to emphasize that contested provinces belonged to the Indonesian cultural sphere like the Dutch colonial government had done in the first half of the twentieth century. Amrin Imran and Syamsuar Said, *Timor Timur: Provinsi ke-27 Republik Indonesia* (Jakarta: Mutiara, 1981); Nyoman Suarjana, *Cerita Rakyat dari Timor Timur* (Jakarta: Gramedia Widiasarana Indonesia, 1993); Sutrisno, *Timor Timur Bersatu Dalam Negara Kesatuan Republik Indonesia* (Semarang: Mandiri Jaya Abadi, 1994). For more general propaganda pieces, see Machmuddin Noor, Slamet Moeljono, Sujamto, and H. Soemarno, *Lahirnya Propinsi Timor Timur* (Jakarta: Almanak Republik Indonesia,1977); Soekanto, Soemanto, Soegeng, Widjono Soekartin, and Karwan, *Integrasi: Kebulatan Tekad Rakyat Timor Timur* (Jakarta: Yayasan Parikesit, 1976). For international audiences, see Department of Information Republic of Indonesia, *East Timor after Integration* (Jakarta: Department of Information Republic of Indonesi, 1983) as well as publications by pro-integration actors like Hendro Subroto, *Eyewitness to Integration of East Timor* (Jakarta: Pustaka Sinar Harapan,1997) and Arsenio Ramos Horta, *The Eyewitness: Bitter moments in East Timor Jungles* (Singapore: Usaha Quality Papers, 1981). For the objective of decolonization and the dilemmas these posed at KAA, see Christopher J. Lee, "Introduction," in *Making a World after Empire: The Bandung Moment and Its Political Afterlives*, ed. Christopher J. Lee (Athens, OH: Ohio University Press, 2010), 7–9; Dipesh Chakrabarty, "The Legacies of Bandung: Decolonization and the Politics of Culture," in Lee, *Making a World*, 45–64. Estêvão Cabral, "The Indonesian Propaganda War against East Timor," in *The East Timor Question: The Struggle for Independence from Indonesia*, ed. Paul Hainsworth and Stephen McCloskey (London: I. B. Tauris Publishers, 2000), 69–84; David Hicks, *Rhetoric and the Decolonization and Recolonization of East Timor* (New York: Routledge, 2015), 64–87; Robinson, *If You Leave Us Here*, 81–84.

[42] PIJAR stands for Pusat Informasi dan Jaringan Aksi Reformasi, LEKHAT for Lembaga Kajian Hak2 Masyarakat. Brief Notes about Indonesian participants, 1–2, in Centro de Intervenção Para o Desenvolvimento Amílcar Cabral (from now on abbreviated as CIDAC), TL 1784.

[43] Janet Steele, "Representations of 'The Nation' in *TEMPO* Magazine," Indonesia 76 (2003): 127, 129, 130; Duncan McCargo, "Killing the Messenger: The 1994 Press Bannings and the Demise of Indonesia's New Order," *Press/Politics* 1, no. 4 (Winter 1999): 29–45; Aditjondro, *Challenges and Prospects*, 1–2.

the New Order regime unwittingly created room for an alternative even more "radical" media landscape.

First, the editors of *Tempo* had moved their news coverage to the vastly expanding World Wide Web earlier that year. *Tempo Interaktif*—as the online version of the magazine was called—was able to outwit the bureaucratic New Order regime and produce content more freely than its printed version was ever allowed to do. But even after escaping the New Order's censorship, the website continued *Tempo*'s earlier trend of limited coverage of the events in East Timor.[44] Moreover, unlike today, few people had Internet access in Indonesia in 1994, and *Tempo Interaktif* could not reach the same audience as its paper predecessor, let alone the more popular *DeTik*, which had a circulation of about 215,000 before being banned.[45] *Tempo*'s chief editor Goenawan Mohamad launched the printed *Independen: forum wartawan* (later renamed *Suara Independen*, in print 1994–95) bulletin that did directly criticize the East Timorese integration and the dubious investments in the "27th province" by Suharto's family.[46] In the previous years, Goenawan's journalists had primarily covered these issues via reports on the legal trials of the younger group of Indonesian activists—including members of PIJAR—or even discussions held in Dutch parliament. Finding themselves banned by the regime, they now adapted this oppositional narrative directly, thereby making the issue more apparent among their remaining readers.[47]

Second, underground publications like *Kabar dari PIJAR* (News from PIJAR) obtained new readership by attracting former subscribers of aforementioned banned magazines. This sudden increase in popularity allowed PIJAR to raise its publication rate and also go online with its own mailing list in early 1996.[48] The samizdat media outlets of PIJAR and LEKHAT made East Timor a topic that was talked about among a growing group of Indonesian activists between 1994 and 1996. Their members often paid the price for this public display of solidarity.

I will illustrate the personal sacrifice and dilemmas faced by this new generation of Indonesian activists by shortly discussing the fate of two PIJAR members: the Indonesian journalist and chief editor of the PIJAR bulletin Tri Agus Susanto Siswowiharjo and the student activist Yenny Rosa Damayanti. Throughout the second half of the year 1994, they frequently reported on protests and the Indonesian government's retaliatory measures against them.[49] Most noticeably, Tri Agus and Yenny were present during the

---

[44] David T. Hill and Krishna Sen, "The Internet in Indonesia's new democracy", Democratization 7.1 (2000), 129–30, 135; David T. Hill, *The Press in New Order Indonesia* (Sheffield, UK: Equinox Publishing, 2006), 13, 49, 72, 88–91, 157; Aditjondro, *Challenges and Prospects*, 7.

[45] Hill, *Press in New Order*, 96–97.

[46] Aditjondro, *Challenges and Prospects*, 7.

[47] Fikri Jufri, Toriq Hadad, Sandra Hamid, and Zed Abidien, "Peristiwa Itu Tak Jatuh dari Langit," *Tempo* (December 7, 1991), 22–25; Ahmed K. Soeriawidjaja and Asbari N. Krisna, "Timor Timur di 'Tweede Kamer,'" *Tempo* (December 7, 1991) 30–31; Toriq Hadad, Bambang Sujatmoko, and Diah Purnomowati, "Sekadar Tikus yang Merepotkan," *Tempo* (December 5, 1992), 22–25; Toriq Hadad, Bambang Sujatmoko, Diah Purnomowati, Zed Abidien, and Dewi Anggraeni, "Loyo Tanpa Xanana?," *Tempo* (December 5, 1992), 26; Bambang Sujatmoko, A. Kukuh Karsadi, and Joewarno, "Mengadili Demonstran Pelesetan," *Tempo* (January 22, 1994), 30; Andi Reza Rohadian, "Hukuman Xanana Gusmao: Surat Xanana, Sanksi Lopa," *Tempo* (January 22, 1994), 31.

[48] Hill and Sen, "The Internet," 129.

[49] David T. Hill, *Pers di Masa Orde Baru* (Jakarta: Pustaka Obor, 2011), vii–iii.

Asia Pacific Conference on East Timor (APCET) in Manilla (May 31–June 4, 1994) where they "insisted that the people of East Timor should have the opportunity to determine their own fate."[50] Just shortly earlier, on May 2, 1994, Xanana had written directly to members of PIJAR that "he considered Indonesians as our brothers and sisters (*povo irmão*), as a neighbouring nation with which many important economic opportunities lay ahead."[51] In 1995, PIJAR published Indonesian translations of a UN report on East Timor and the defense plea of the imprisoned leader of RENETIL Fernando de Araújo. For the first time, Indonesian audiences were able to engage with the particularities of the occupation of East Timor and were confronted with claims to human right abuses that had been common in Anglophone and other Western media for numerous years already.

The New Order regime responded to these translations by arresting Tri Agus for having "insulted" President Suharto a year earlier in an article quoting a prominent Indonesian activist who protested against the ban of the three aforementioned weeklies.[52] The head of PIJAR, Nuku Soleiman (1965–2003), had been convicted a year earlier for "offending the president" during a demonstration in November 1993.[53] Tri Agus was first kept at Salemba Prison, Jakarta, where he came to attract international attention after being designated as a "prisoner of conscience" by Amnesty International. This also improved his status among Indonesian followers. To his European correspondents, he quipped that he was able to continue his activism by luring philatelists from all over Java to his cell with the postage stamps taken from the thousands of letters received from the other side of the world. Prison, he wrote from inside his cell in Salemba Prison, made me an "optimistic man . . . I have received many thinkings of peace and human rights from abroad through correspondence [sic]."[54]

Tri Agus's prison sentence reshaped his political agenda even more fundamentally when he was transferred to Cipinang Prison halfway through the year 1996. He was placed in the same prison block as Xanana, with whom be became close friends.[55] Once the authorities found out, they decided to move Tri Agus to Semarang to prevent further unity between the parties. But this was to no avail. When Tri Agus was released on March 10, 1997, he announced to Amnesty International and other Western media that he would continue "his struggle to bring democracy and human rights to Indonesia and

---

[50] Lane, *Indonesian Solidarity*, 24.

[51] Xanana Gusmão, *Letter to PIJAR's chairman Rachland Nashidik and Other Members of PIJAR* (Cipinang Jakarta, May 2, 1994), 1, in CIDAC, TL 7082.

[52] This Indonesian activist was the lawyer Adnan Buyung Nasution who claimed that "this country has been thrown into a mess by someone called Suharto." Aditjondro, *Challenges and Prospects*, 3; Tri Agus Susanto Siswowiharjo, *From Prison with Peace and Love* (May 6, 1996), 3, in ISSG, ARCH02325.49, 54.

[53] Comissão para os Direitos do Povo Maubere, *Timor Leste* XI.114 (Lisbon: CDPM, 1995), 3; Conselho Nacional Da Resistencia Maubere (CNRM), *Retaliação das forças policiais indonésias sobre os participantes da Operação "HAMUTUK" de 7 de Dezembro de 1995: Press release* (Jakarta: CNRM, 1996), 1; Cees van Dijk, "The Partai Demokrasi Indonesia," *Bijdragen tot de Taal- , Land- en Volkenkunde* 153, no. 3 (1997): 409, 417–22, 429; Aditjondro, *Challenges and Prospects*, 6; Cornelis Dijk and Kees van Dijk, *A Country in Despair: Indonesia Between 1997 and 2000* (Leiden: KITLV Press, 2001), 22; L. Rama M, *Indonésia, o império em decadência / intervenção do Presidio do Conselho Central da RENETIL* (Oporto: RENETIL 1996), 3–4.

[54] Tri Agus recalls having received over 3,500 letters from the Netherlands, Belgium, Germany, Australia, New Zealand, Spain, the United States, Japan, England, and Ireland between his imprisonment in 1995 and March 1996. Siswowiharjo, *From Prison*, 4, 13–14 (55, 59–60).

[55] Interview with Tri Agus Susanto Siswowiharjo, March 28, in the restaurant of the Puri Artha hotel in Yogyakarta.

East Timor."[56] A year later, he joined SOLIDAMOR (Solidarity for Peaceful Resolution for East Timor[57]) as campaign division manager, and started working on new series of translations and original publications that would reinvigorate the Indonesian debate on whether the New Order had committed human right violations. Simultaneously, Tri Agus and SOLIDAMOR's chairperson Bonar Tigor "Coky" Naipospos reemphasized the diplomatic harm that Indonesia inflicted on itself by continuing the seemingly never-ending conflict in "Tim-Tim." They warned that whereas Suharto enjoyed full support from the governments of Australia and the United States in 1975 due to the potential oil profits, this had turned around in the following decades.[58]

Tri Agus' colleague from PIJAR, Yenny, had gone through a similar development in prison. By the time she got out in 1995, she had obtained a broad international audience that, on its turn, also allowed her to also to attract attention within Indonesian media. Still, Yenny's case shows that the spotlight was a curse too which in her case led to numerous years of exile. Her eviction started at a Portuguese and German conference to which she was invited shortly after her release from prison.

Portuguese Conferences

Yenny was invited to Europe by a professor of engineering who had served on the staff of the last Portuguese colonial governor of East Timor. Prof Barbedo de Magalhães had become one of the most significant figures within the Portuguese-East Timor Solidarity movement by the mid-1990s.[59] He wanted Indonesian activists to participate in European fora to make EU governments better aware that East Timor was symptomatic of a much larger and more pressing issue—Suharto's dictatorship and its suppression of Indonesian and East Timorese populations throughout the archipelago.[60] For instance, he drew attention to the efforts of the Indonesian student activist Yenny Rosa Damayanti,

[56] Amnesty International, "Indonesia and East Timor: Tri Agus, 'I'm Never Going to Shut Up,'" *Amnesty International News*, March 22, 1998, Index Number: NWS 22/04/98.

[57] SOLIDAMOR is a portmanteau of Solidaritas untuk Penyelesaian Damai Timor Timur and cooperated closely with the Forum Solidaritas untuk rakyat Timor Timur (FORTILOS). "Ensiklotimor: FORTILOS," *Solid* 6 (1999), 32.

[58] Unlike Tri Agus, SOLIDAMOR's chairman, Bonar Tigor Naipospos (born: Jakarta, October 13, 1957), had been imprisoned in Wirogunan prison in Yogyakarta. Pakpahan, *Mengenal Timor*; José Ramos-Horta, *Funu: perjuangan Timor lorosae belum selesai* (Jakarta: SOLIDAMOR, 1998); Xanana Gusmão, *Timor Leste merdeka, Indonesia bebas* (Jakarta: SOLIDAMOR, 1998); Siswowihardjo, *Mati Ketawa*; Andriyanto, ed., *Pasukan pembunuh Indonesia: membunuh tanpa dihukum, kronologi kekejaman kelompok paramiliter dan milisi yang disponsori oleh Militer Indonesia di Timor Timur dari Nopember 1998 sampai Mei 1999* (Jakarta: SOLIDAMOR, 1998); George Junus Aditjondro, *Tangan-tangan berlumuran minyak: politik minyak di balik tragedi Timor Lorosae* (Jakarta: SOLIDAMOR, 2000); Bonar Tigor Naipospos, "Tidak ada Tentara yang senang di Timor Timur," *Solid* 2 (December 1998), 21; SOLIDAMOR, "Hubungan Indonesia—Australia Paska Jajak Pendapat dit Timor Timur," *Solid* 6 (1999), 23; SOLIDAMOR, "SOLIDAMOR: Solidarity without Border" (Jakarta: SOLIDAMOR, 2000), in CIDAC, TL5461.

[59] After Portugal had joined the EU in 1985, and Mário Soares was elected President in 1986 (he was reelected by a landslide in 1991 for a second five-year term) Portugal began to play a much more proactive role on the East Timor issue, defending the inalienable right of the East Timorese to decide their political fate through a UN-supervised referendum.

[60] Antonio Barbedo de Magalhães, *The East Timor Issue and the Symposia of Oporto University* (Porto: Universidade do Porto, May 19, 1995), 40–56; "Silence and Democracy: Women's Liberation, Independence Is Not Enough: Open Letter to Prof. António Barbedo de Magalhães" (sent from VI *Jornadas* in East Timor on March 20, 1995)

Plate 1 Left: The image of Yenny that Prof. Barbedo de Magalhães printed in his overview of conferences held on the Solidarity movement in Lisbon with the caption "Indonesian youth is also struggling for freedom" to advertise the conference on Indonesian activists that he would organize on February 22–24, 1996. Right: Yenny on the cover of a contemporary edition of the GATRA news magazine (April 29, 1995) asking: "WHY HAVE THEY BEEN ACCUSED? [KENAPA MEREKA DITUDUH?]"[61]

whom he invited to the conference held between February 22–24, 1996: just months after her release from prison in Jakarta. Her invitation to Lisbon led to another conference invitation this time in Germany. At that point, information reached her from friends in Indonesia that she would be rearrested if she returned to Indonesia. She promptly packed her bags, took the night train, and moved to the Netherlands to claim political asylum. As she entered the Netherlands, she found that the New Order had already canceled her Indonesian passport. She remained stateless for the next two years (1996–98).[62]

Despite the surveillance of the Indonesian intelligence services, the Lisbon-Oporto conferences were of great significance. Among other things, they aimed to highlight the contribution of the Indonesian solidarity movement to East Timor's fight for freedom

---

[61] Barbedo de Magalhães, *Symposia of Oporto* University, 55.

[62] Her passport would only be revived three days after the fall of Suharto in 1998. Interview with Yenny Rosa Damayanti, June 25, 2020, via WhatsApp. Yenny Rosa Damayanti is a former member of the aforementioned PIJAR and SOLIDAMOR.

since the early 1990s.[63] Most important, they raised the international profile of Indonesian involvement in the transnational solidarity movement, only a few months after a public forum in Sydney had first brought together Indonesian as well as East Timorese activists who strived for self-determination of East Timor.[64] This contributed to the ever louder calls for East Timorese self-determination in both the West and Indonesia itself. In 1992, Professor Barbedo had already proclaimed that "the demonstrations of Indonesian students against the [Santa Cruz and other East Timor] massacres; their protests against Jakarta's occupation of East Timor, together with their campaign for the democratization of the Indonesian regime" were of "special importance" to the solidarity movement at-large.[65] He took this message to heart. One veteran Indonesian activist, the TAPOL member Liem Sioe Liong, expressed strong appreciated for the "Porto conference" of 1995 in a letter addressed to Prof. Barbedo on March 1, 1996, underscoring how they bolstered the solidarity movement at large and helped to unite Indonesian activists of widely different backgrounds:

> The opportunity for Indonesian democrats to exchange thoughts with Timorese, the international community and the Portuguese public is really invaluable. The Indonesians go back home with the feeling of being part of an international network and strengthened in the[ir] political convictions about the just demands of the East Timorese.[66]

This was a powerful statement from an activist who himself had been exiled from Indonesia after joining the Permanent People's Tribunal in Lisbon in 1981.[67] Indeed, University of Oporto expended its conferences to Sydney on June 21–24, 1996 to attract even more East Timorese and Indonesian speakers from a wider range of activist groups.[68] But the positive note with which Liem ended his letter would soon prove misplaced. Within days of its dispatch, Yenny would be knocking on his door in Amsterdam looking for a hideout from the Indonesian secret service.[69] All Indonesian citizens who dared to question Suharto came under suspicion and pressure, many suffering long jail terms and torture. This was as true in 1996 as it had been for Liem fifteen years earlier.

Dictatorships have long memories and the situation was particularly tense during the Lisbon-Oporto conference of 1996 as it took place just two months after an event that

[63] The international conference "Solidariedade da juventude indonésia, esperança para Timor Leste" was organized by Barbedo de Magalhães in Lisbon on February 22–24, 1996. Unfortunately, it was held during the celebrations of the Muslim New Year (Hari Raya Idulfitri), causing some invited Muslim activists to decline their invitations so as not to miss the celebrations at home in Indonesia. Wilson, *The Indonesian Pro-Democracy Movement*; António Barbedo de Magalhães, *Solidariedade da juventude indonesia, esperança para Timor Leste: Conferência Internacional 22 a 24 de fevereiro de 1996* (Porto: Universidade do Porto, 1996); António Barbedo de Magalhães, *Ministro dos Negócios Estrangeiros: Timor Leste* (Porto: Universidade do Porto, 1996); Liem Soei Liong, "Closing Session East Timor Conference, Lisbon 24 Febr. 1996," *Solidariedade da juventude indonésia, esperança para Timor Leste: Conferência Internacional* (Porto: University of Porto, 1996), 1.

[64] Lane, *Indonesian Solidarity*, 23.

[65] António Barbedo de Magalhães, *Timor-Leste ocupacao Indonesia e genocidio com conivencia internacional* (Oporto: University of Oporto, January 22, 1992), 34.

[66] Liem Soei Liong, [letter to] António Barbedo Magalhães (Amsterdam, March 1, 1996), 1.

[67] Liem Soei Liong, "Closing Session East Timor Conference, Lisbon 24 Febr. 1996," *Solidariedade da juventude indonésia, esperança para Timor Leste: Conferência Internacional* (Oporto: University of Porto, 1996), 1.

[68] Lane, *Indonesian Solidarity*, 24.

[69] Interview with Liem Soei Liong, February 12, 2020, in his house in central Amsterdam.

forever revolutionized the relationship between Timorese and Indonesian activists. In many ways, this so-called Operation Hamutuk was the apex of the cooperation that had been initiated by Xanana three years earlier. It brought together PRD and RENETIL and established a cooperation that gave an extra layer of meaning to the interaction occurring between Indonesian and Timorese activists in international conferences. One Indonesian history graduate who had also presented at the Lisbon-Oporto conference in February 1996 played an important role in these developments.

SPRIM

RENETIL's approaches to PRD led to the founding of the Indonesian Peoples' Solidarity Struggle with the Maubere People (SPRIM) in March 1995 under its coordinator, Wilson bin Nurtyas.[70] As one of the editors of the Legal Aid Institute (LBH)'s *Jurnal Demokrasi* and head of the Department of Education and Propaganda of PDI, the fresh history graduate Wilson was a labor rights advocate who decided to extend his activism to victims of Suharto's military operations. As his press release during his trial in June 1997 stretches: "the problem of East Timor should become the problem of Indonesians [for] our constitution and anti-colonial foundation have to be cherished and remembered by the people."[71] Wilson's personal archive proves that this decision was a strategic one. During a public meeting on East Timor in Sydney—to which Wilson had been invited after his release from prison on July 27, 1998—he stated:

> [Recent developments show] there has been an opening up of political space—not just in Indonesia but also in East Timor, where there have been huge mobilisations in Dili and other cities demanding self-determination. This proves that the tactic of linking the fight for democracy in Indonesia and the struggle for self-determination in East Timor is a correct one.[72]

By that time, he could look back at three years of campaigning, most of it conducted from prison, in which he had successfully managed to draw the attention of foreign (mainly Anglo- and Lusophone) supporters.

Wilson's engagement with East Timor took shape in 1995 at the same point in time that the New Order regime decided to take a firm stance against the Indonesian activists for their actions aimed at promoting Democratic reform and improving working conditions for Indonesian laborers. Importantly, however, the SPRIM activists framed their support for East Timor in such a way that it appeared as if it happened simultaneously with the increase of international attention on the conflict following the tapes of the 1991 Santa Cruz massacre. In an article written on November 12, 1997—six years after the massacre occurred—Wilson states that it was this event that "opened my eyes to ABRI's (Indonesian armed forces) despicable brutality in East Timor."[73] It is

---

[70] SPRIM stands for Solidaritas Perjuangan Rakyat Indonesia Untuk Maubere. Wilson, *The Indonesian Pro-Democracy Movement*.

[71] Wilson bin Nurtyas, *Siaran Pers: Pembelaan Politik Dalam Persidangan Aktivis Partai Rakyat Demokratik* (LP Cipinang, Jakarta, June 10, 1997), ISSG, ARCH02712, 2005; Aspinall, *Opposing Suharto*, 282.

[72] Wilson bin Nurtyas, "Indonesia: 'The Struggle Must Be Completed," ed. James Balowski, *Green Left Weekly* 344 (1998), 3.

[73] Wilson bin Nurtyas, "Behind Bar," Asian Human Rights Commission, Newsletter 8, no. 1 (1998): 1–2. ARCH02712 [originally written on November 12, 1997, published in English on January 1, 1998]. Similar

noticeable, however, that the first vigil against the massacre and ongoing bloodshed that was organized by Wilson and his peers occurred only two years earlier and that Wilson would later contradict himself by elaborating how Princen had introduced him to the issue and dilemmas of East Timor in 1995.[74]

The Santa Cruz Massacre did not instantaneously change the debate on East Timor within Indonesia. In a recent article, Takahiro points at the response of senior Indonesian intellectuals like Seno Gumira Ajidarma and George Aditjondro to conclude that, in the wake of the event, "East Timorese nationalists amalgamated with pro-democracy youths in Indonesia to further crystalize their cause in the Indonesian context."[75] But this simplifies the slow process at which young Indonesian activists became familiar with the massacre.

Nothing in the archives and publications of the younger generation of Indonesian (student) activists indicates that Santa Cruz was a key concern for them between 1991 and 1994. By 1995, this had clearly changed. The Indonesian solidarity movement was not already fully shaped in the aftermath of the Santa Cruz Massacre. Instead, it took four years before East Timor became a major goal of the Indonesian protest movement. This is not surprising given how little information on East Timor reached Java and Sumatra and how dangerous it was to discuss the occupation openly. Only by the end of 1995—in the wake of the ongoing prosecution of PRD members by the New Order regime, which would soon culminate in its complete ban—did the struggle for East Timorese self-determination become a "significant strategic opportunity for those seeking change in Indonesia."[76] It did so, as Wilson emphasizes, through the influence of Poncke Princen who offered aid to the students when they found themselves in dire straits.

This sea of change reflected the increased cooperation between a new generation of Indonesian and Timorese activists in Jakarta and the wider solidarity movement abroad. The Santa Cruz Massacre mattered to audiences and solidarity movements abroad and could therefore be leveraged to gain their support. Until then, protesting against the East Timorese occupation would have likely come at the cost of other more prominent aims like higher minimal wages or democratic reform within Indonesia. The crackdown on the PRD turned the tables around; cornered by the regime, the party struggled to organize strikes and demonstrations and needed a new channel to project their political aims. Soon after, Wilson and his peers also grew disappointed with the leadership of Megawati, who—writes Wilson—had failed "to make use of the positive sides of the [July 27, 1996] incident to improve the quality of her struggle."[77] The last group they could turn to was the international solidarity movement.

The young 1990s generation of Indonesian activists quickly learned to catch world attention for their various humanitarian causes. East Timor, which had remained throughout an international issue by virtue of its status as a non-decolonized territory, was key here. The very public horror of the Santa Cruz massacre greatly enhanced its

claims were made by SOLIDAMOR in their *Solid* magazine, see, for instance, "Ensiklotimor: Dili," *Solid* 4 (May 1999), 45.

[74] Wilson, "Poncke Princen"; Adam, "Tokoh Langka."

[75] Takahiro, "Beyond Nationalism," 86–88.

[76] Robinson, *If You Leave Us Here*, 84–85; Webster, "Non-State Diplomacy," 24.

[77] Wilson, "Behind Bar," 2.

status as an international cause célèbre. Through meetings and debates with RENETIL, these Indonesian activist groups learned how to use the cause of East Timor to put their own political agenda in the global spotlight.

Operation Hamutuk

Once the relationship between Indonesian and Timorese student activists had become firmly established in mid-1995, Gusmão, from his Cipinang jail cell, began planning a joint campaign to draw the world's attention to the new Indonesian-Timorese alliances. These efforts resulted in "Operation Hamutuk," the temporary occupation of the Dutch and Russian embassies in Jakarta and simultaneous campus protests throughout Java and Bali. The operation took place on December 7, 1995—the twentieth anniversary of the Indonesian invasion of East Timor. At this point of time in 1995, the main Indonesian solidarity members were still out in the open, their actions being limited to making verbal statements. Operation Hamutuk changed all this. Henceforth, their involvement in the struggle for East Timorese self-determination would be irrevocably linked to the demand for democratic reform in Indonesia at large. The human costs of this operation were considerable. Many Indonesian and Timorese members of the Jakarta-based solidarity movement became marked individuals, relentlessly pursued by Indonesian intelligence and security forces. Those that failed to escape the dragnet were arrested and sent to prison in the months following the operation.[78]

Operation Hamutuk sought to draw the attention of the UN Human Rights Special Representative, the Ecuadorian lawyer and diplomat Dr. José Ayala Lasso, who was visiting the Indonesian capital that very day.[79] During the past two years, there had been numerous sit-ins in embassies conducted by East Timorese students studying on Java. The Indonesian government portrayed these sit-ins as opportunistic actions by the students who—it claimed—sought asylum overseas to improve their personal well-being. Indeed, many did try to find a way out of the misery caused by the Indonesian occupation by going abroad. Usually only about five to twelve Timorese students were involved in these actions, but Operation Hamutuk included almost ninety activists to prove the point that occupying embassies was not about getting visas but rather to obtain international attention for real political causes.[80]

A few hours before the opening time of the Dutch embassy, twenty-six East Timorese and twenty-nine SPRIM activists climbed over "the vertical metal rungs of the fence and jumped over the roll of barbed wire" to enter the compound.[81] At 8 a.m., Wilson (SPRIM),

[78] Rei, *Resistance*, 148, 200, 211–14; Oosttimorezen opnieuw belaagd, "Oosttimorezen opniew belaags," *Het Parool* (December 12, 1995). See also Angie Bexley and Nuno Rodrigues Tchailoro, "Consuming Youth: Timorese in the Resistance against Indonesian Occupation," *The Asia Pacific Journal of Anthropology* 14, no. 5 (2013): 413.

[79] Conselho Nacional Da Resistencia Maubere (CNRM), *Retaliação das forças policiais indonésias sobre os participantes da Operação "HAMUTUK" de 7 de Dezembro de 1995: Press release* (Jakarta: CNRM, 1996), 1.

[80] Fernandes, Clinton. 2011. *Independence of East Timor: Multi-Dimensional perspectives -Occupation, Resistance, and International Political Activism*. Sussex Academic press: 136–7; Lane, *Indonesian Solidarity*, 22–23; Gusmão, *A Woman of Independence*, 145–48.

[81] The action started at 3 a.m., around 4 a.m., the Timorese and Indonesian activists had entered the compound of the Dutch embassy. Around 7 a.m., they were approached by a member of the embassy staff to clarify their actions. Within an hour of this conversation, they were able to meet the Dutch Ambassador and

Petrus Haryanto (PS-PRD), and Naldo Rei (RENETIL) met the Dutch ambassador, Paul Brouwer, in person. Brouwer was forthcoming and willing to direct all their demands of action to the Dutch government.[82] He also helped them contact international bodies like the United Nations, the International Red Cross, the aforementioned H. J. Princen, and even directly called the Indonesian Foreign Minister, Ali Alatas, who quickly hung up to avoid any contact with the activists. Lasso was equally hesitant and only sent his junior representative to talk to the group. The Red Cross—staying true to its founding statement of being a neutral body—refused to get involved in the action altogether. Still, Princen did come and so did the journalists. The first joint action of the Indonesian-Timorese thus seemingly turned into a media success, even though some of the participants were arrested and tortured by the New Order regime at the end of the occupation, and others involved with the organizing of the demonstration needed to flee abroad.[83]

The apparent success of Operation Hamutuk belies the fact that the coordination between SPRIM and the Timorese students was still undermined by internal distrust. Princen urged the activists to cease their occupation, apparently knowing that the regime was planning to use this to depict the activists as being disunited.[84] One of the Timorese organizers of the operation—Naldo Rei—recalled how his "comrades" were suspicious of the Indonesians involved: "The way they saw it, Indonesians were the same as ABRI [the Indonesian army] who so enjoyed killing the Maubere people. . . . In the end I swore to them that I would be prepared for them to kill me if SPRIM betrayed us."[85]

Overcoming the tensions between Indonesian and Timorese activists was crucial to Naldo Rei for the same reasons that involving Indonesian activists had been on the agenda of Prof. Barbedo in Portugal. Rei argued that direct Indonesian involvement "would help to challenge the government propaganda about their generous development of my country. It would expand the struggle and its resolution outside isolated East Timor to Indonesia itself."[86] The black banner unfolded in the Dutch embassy yard on December 7, 1995 made his convictions all too clear, it read: "FREE INDONESIA [AND] EAST TIMOR!"

The banner was a red flag for the irregular troops of the Indonesian General and Suharto's son-in-law, the very recently (December 1, 1995) appointed Kopassus (Indonesian Special Forces) commander, Lieutenant-General Prabowo Subianto Djojohadikusumo, who had gathered outside of the embassy. On Prabowo's orders, they

unfold their banners within the compound. Rei, *Resistance*, 205; Takahiro, "Beyond Nationalism," 77, Naldo Rei, *Timor Timur: Sebuah Memoar* (Jakarta: Circa, 2017), 168–69; Gusmão, *A Woman of Independence*, 147–48.

[82] Rei, *Resistance*, 205.

[83] Brouwer had apparently already signed a petition for Timorese self-determination of the Parliamentary Human Rights Group in 1983, see UK House of Commons., Parliamentary Human Rights Group, *Parliamentarians of 8 EEC countries call for East Timor self-determination: Press Release* (London: Parliamentary Human Rights Group, 1983), 5; Rei, *Resistance*, 205–6, 211; M. L. Vos, *International Cooperation between Politics and Practice: How Dutch Indonesian Cooperation Changed Remarkably Little after a Diplomatic Rupture* (Amsterdam: University of Amsterdam, 2001). See also Irena Cristalis, *East Timor: A Nation's Bitter Dawn* (London: Zed Books, 2009), 25; Gusmão, *A Woman of Independence*, 148–62.

[84] Rei, *Resistance*, 210–11; Rei, *Timor Timur*, 172–73.

[85] The Timorese deserter ran after rumors spread that the army had surrounded the RENETIL base on the eve of the operation. The alarm, however, turned out to have been set off by a security guard who did his nightly rounds around the complex, see Rei, *Resistance*, 203–4.

[86] Rei, *Resistance*, 204.

too jumped over the embassy fence at 10 a.m. on December 7 to assault the activists. Prabowo had mustered these "pro-integrationists"—or "tugs" as Naldo Rei calls them—from eastern Indonesia and even East Timor as part of his Young Guards for the Upholding of Integration (Gardapaksi).[87] Their Timorese appearance made this assault look like an internal scuffle between the Indonesian and Timorese activists.

According to Naldo Rei, they were paid the meagre sum of 15,000 Rupiah (approximately three Australian dollars) to cause havoc with daggers, metal pipes, and rocks with the cameras of the Indonesian press rolling. It seems more likely, however, that they were already integrated into the Indonesian military hierarchy before the event and guided by the conviction that the Indonesian Integration of East Timor was a worthy cause.[88] Bloodshed was avoided when Brouwer quickly stepped in and ordered the activists to enter the building while the intruders were shown the door. Later that afternoon, the assailants returned to lay siege to the embassy with their own banners while chanting "One Land, One Nation" (Satu Nusa Satu Bangsa); a phrase derived from the Youth Pledge made by young Indonesian nationalists in 1928—and later reworked into an anthem in 1947—which was considered to be seminal to the national awakening by Sukarno as well as Suharto.[89] The next morning at 10 a.m., the assailants entered the embassy and injured Paul Brouwer, who tried to stop them from jumping on Naldo Rei. Brouwer needed to be brought to the hospital instantly. This attack on a top diplomat greatly increased international pressure on the Indonesian-affiliated forces, but this did not hinder the regime to send in three hundred armed police and military officers the next day to arrest the activists.[90]

On that faithful morning of December 9, the Indonesian unit commander directly pressured Brouwer in his own office to forsake his diplomatic protection of the activists.[91] But the Indonesian breach of the Vienna Convention on diplomatic immunity backfired and was met by a concerted international outcry, which forced the military regional command to release the Indonesian and Timorese activists the following day.[92] This short burst of violence demonstrates how internal discords between the Indonesian and East Timorese activists, as encountered by Naldo Rei in the preparation of Operation Hamatuk, could easily be exploited by the Indonesian army. At the same time, it also underlines how Indonesian generals needed to be careful in their tactics to undermine their opponents through manipulation as the world was watching.

---

[87] Gardapaksi stands for Garda Muda Penegak Integrasi. Liem Soei Liong, "Closing Session East Timor Conference, Lisbon 24 Febr. 1996," *Solidariedade da juventude indonésia, esperança para Timor Leste: Conferência Internacional* (Oporto: University of Porto, 1996), 2.

[88] Prabowo Subianto Djojohadikusumo was approached for this article, and he personally agreed to an interview, but the 2020–21 COVID-19 pandemic kept it from occurring. He did state to treat all his men—whether regular or irregular—in a similar way. This shows the complexity of the Indonesian army and its parallel hierarchies of which the peripheral elements cannot always be classified as vigilantes in the conventional sense. Gusmão, *A Woman of Independence*, 150–51.

[89] Rei, *Resistance*, 206–7.

[90] Rei, *Timor Timur*, 170–72.

[91] Rei, *Resistance*, 208–10.

[92] Of course, the activists were followed by Intelligence officers after leaving the police station and still ran the risk of being abducted. They escaped this fate by jumping into one of the sewer-like rivers running through Jakarta, after which they made their way to the house of a Jesuit priest in Depok. Rei, meanwhile, hid in Kirsty Sword's residence the day after, see Rei, *Resistance*, 212–14.

Plate 2: The banners unfolded at the Dutch embassy in Jakarta on December 8, 1995.
Photo taken by the Indonesian activist Petrus Hariyanto. See Carlos da Silva and L. F. R.
Saky, RENETIL *Iha Luta Libertasaun* Timor Lorosa'e: Antes sem Título, do que sem Pátria!
(Dili: RENETIL, 2013).

Through Operation Hamutuk, the association between democratic reform and East
Timor motivated other secessionist movements also started to copy the rhetoric of the
Indonesian solidarity movement. For instance, the Free Aceh Movement (Gerakan Aceh
Merdeka, GAM) leader Hasan di Tiro (1925–2010) and his right-hand Muhamad Nur
Djuly—who was the GAM negotiator in the 2005 MOU talks in Helsinki—advocated
the East Timorese cause to bolster their own struggle for self-determination.[93] The
protest action was only part of the reasons why GAM came to embrace RENETIL's
struggle *and* tactics. The other was that when some of the participants of the embassy
jumping were imprisoned many months later, they had already established their
media profiles and—like Tri Agus and Yenny before them—were quickly designated
as "prisoners of conscience" reputedly fighting for the same human rights that were
cherished in Europe.

---

[93] Interview Liem S. Liong. Amsterdam. February 2, 2020

The themes of their protests and the media attention these attracted turned activists like Wilson into martyrs to foreign journalists, whereas many of the Acehnese protestors remained ignored. The activists of SOLIDAMOR were therefore keen to extend their agenda to include Acehnese and Papuan movements within the framework of human rights violations. But they only did so after Suharto had fallen from grace.[94] By that time, the Indonesian and East Timorese activists who were involved with East Timor had already established media profiles in Western documentaries, blogs, and weeklies that could not be matched by GAM members.[95]

United behind Bars: The Cipinang Prison

The banning of the PRD and its branches—including SPRIM—and arrest of eighteen PRD members following the New Order regime's effort to oust Megawati from the head office of the Indonesian Democratic Party on July 27, 1996 incident led to a new cooperation between Wilson and RENETIL, but this time behind bars.[96] Naldo Rei managed to flee the country after operation Hamutuk had ended, but Wilson was eventually arrested and found himself in the company of other East Timorese activists who had not been as lucky. Ironically—and despite the hardships faced while behind bars—the custodial sentences proved a blessing in disguise. Within the space of a brief two years (1996–98), they brought an older and younger generation of both Timorese and Indonesian activists together in a way that would have been impossible otherwise.

This prison was one of the many penitentiary institutions in which Suharto's political opponents were incarcerated.[97] Alongside murderers and burglars it housed dozens of leftists, hardline Islamists, and secessionist activists. Through the assistance of Timorese students—whom they met during visiting hours—the activist prisoners were able to communicate with each other by sending letters from one cell to another, even between separate prison blocks.[98] The Indonesian students and journalists suddenly found themselves in close vicinity of the main East Timorese leaders. Wilson took on the role of chronicler of Xanana's activities during these crucial years prior to the Timorese referendum.[99] Meanwhile, the PRD leader, Budiman Sudjatmiko, also arrested on July

---

[94] Meki Sukasah, "Demokratisasi di Indonesia dan Masa Depan Timor Timur," *Solid* 3 (1999), 7; SOLIDAMOR, "SOLIDAMOR," 3–8.

[95] See footnote 104.

[96] Conselho Nacional Da Resistencia Maubere (CNRM), *Retaliação das forças policiais indonésias sobre os participantes da Operação "HAMUTUK" de 7 de Dezembro de 1995: Press Release* (Jakarta: CNRM, 1996), 1; Roy Pakpahan, *Mengenal Timor Timur: Dulu & Sekarang* (Jakarta: SOLIDAMOR, 1998), 47, 53–54, 69.

[97] James T. Siegel, "Early Thoughts on the Violence of May 13 and 14, 1998 in Jakarta," *Indonesia* 66 (April 1998), 76.

[98] RENETIL, *National Resistance of the Students of East Timor (RENETIL)* (1995), 1, in CIDAC, TL 2822.

[99] As Hariyanto later recalled: "Sometimes chairs were used by Wilson to type while sitting on the floor. He was typing almost every night, even when it was just one or two sheets. He often recorded the daily activities of Xanana. He even noted down whether Xanana had taken a shower or not. He always wrote two copies, one of which was on carbon paper. One of the copies was sent out of jail [to the PRD headquarters in Jakarta], the other to Mrs. Carmel Budiardjo of TAPOL in London," translated by Pocut Hanifah, Petrus Hariyanto, "Memori Kamar No 3 di LP Cipinang," Kisah-Kisah di Balik Penjara, Facebook, May 27, 2020, https://www.facebook.com/Kisah-Kisah-Di-Balik-Penjara-424891551395780/?epa=SEARCH_BOX; Wilson bin Nurtyas, *Xanana by Wilson: Cipinang Prison, October - November 1997*, trans. Charlie Scheiner (New York: ETAN, 1997); Tri Agus Susanto Siswowiharjo, *Mati Ketawa Cara Timor Leste* (Jakarta: SOLIDAMOR, 2002); Wilson bin Nurtyas, *Dunia Di Balik Jeruji: Kesaksian Perlawanan* (Jakarta: Resist Book, 2005).

27, 1996, and his general secretary Petrus Hariyanto were locked up with Fernando de Araújo.[100] The aforementioned Princen was a regular visitor too and contacts were maintained with Liem in Amsterdam and Carmel Budiardjo in London.[101]

These reports and letters from jail all served a single purpose; the struggle for public recognition of the solidarity movement as a whole, which in this penitentiary setting ranged from the old to the new generation of Timorese and Indonesian activists. Journalists of the *Green Left* weekly, ABC Australia, and even Indonesian journalists reported on their lives in prison, and staff from Amnesty International kept an eye on their well-being.[102] The fact that they kept in touch with the rest of the world from inside the panopticon of the New Order itself owed much to a single Indonesian sympathizer of the democratic cause: the Cipinang prison director, Mohamad Sobari. Sobari allowed the detained activists and reformists to exchange letters, obtain typewriters, hold events, and communicate with the outside world.[103] Despite being part of the New Order administration by virtue of being a public servant, his loyalty toward Suharto wavered after the latter had fallen out of grace up to the point that he admitted to Xanana that "if I had a say in the matter, I would not hesitate in releasing all of you political prisoners today."[104] In 1998/99, nearly all Indonesian and East Timorese activists in Cipinang were

---

[100] Petrus Hariyanto, Kisah-Kisah di Balik Penjara, Facebook group, May 20, 2019–ongoing; Arsénio Paixão Bano, Quintiliano Mok, and Jean Pierre Korreman, *National Resistance of the Students of East Timor (RENETIL)* (Lisbon: RENETIL, 1995), 1.

[101] Naldo Rei, *Resistance*, 205–6.

[102] Nico Warouw, "Indonesian Prisoners Announce Hunger Strike", *Green Left Weekly* 265 (March 5, 1997); Melanie Sjoberg, "Suharto Will Have to Jail All the Youth," *Green Left Weekly* 277 (June 4, 1997); John Roosa, "The View from Cipinang Prison," *Green Left Weekly* 282 (July 23, 1997); Kylie Moon, "Two Political Prisoners Released," *Green Left Weekly* (March 4, 1998), 308; "Cipinang Prison Football Team," *Green Left Weekly* 312 (April 1, 1998); James Balowsky, "PRD Prisoners Released," *Green Left Weekly* 326 (July 29, 1998); Max Lane, "Court Un-bans PRD, but Harassment Continues," *Green Left Weekly* 330 (August 26, 1998); "Xanana Denies BHP Meeting," *Green Left Weekly* 333 (August 26, 1998); Tuntuni Bhattacharyya, "Dita Sari Interview Smuggled from Prison," *Green Left Weekly* 338 (October 28, 1998); Wilson bin Nurtyas, "Indonesia: 'The Struggle Must Be Completed," ed. James Balowski, *Green Left Weekly* 344 (1998), 3; James Balowski, "Indonesian Regime Backtracking on Budiman Release?," *Green Left Weekly* 353 (March 17, 1999); Sam King, "Dita Sari Is Free!," *Green Left Weekly* 368 (July 21, 1999); Max Lane, "PRD Leader Anom Astika Released," *Green Left Weekly* 370 (August 4, 1999); ABC Australia, *An Activist Silenced*. Produced by ABC Australia, May 1, 1997, Journeyman Pictures, https://www.journeyman.tv/film/344/an-activist-silenced; Jill Hickson, *There Is Only One Word, RESIST*, coproduced and distributed by Actively Radical TV (ARTV) and Action in Solidarity with Indonesia and East Timor (ASIET), 1997, https://youtu.be/dlXGNfCChyI; Jill Hickson and John Reynolds, *Indonesia in Revolt: Democracy or Death*, coproduced by ASIET and ARTV, 1998, https://youtu.be/NhYd3zmRd14; ISSG, ARCH02712_2005; Dita Sari, *Letter to Wilson* (Rutan klas I surabaya [medaeng], May 27, 1997), in ISSG, ARCH02712_2005.

[103] Al-Chaidar, *Sepak Terjang KW IX, Abu Toto Syaikh A.S. Pandji Gumilang Menyelewengkan NKA-NII Pasca S.M. Kartosuwirjo* (Jakarta: Madani Press, 200), 100; Farid Junaedi, *Memanusiakan Manusia Pilihan: Sebuah Catatan Singkat Petugas yang Biasa Disebut "Sipir"* (Jakarta: Deepublish, 2017), 61; Sri Bintang Pamungkas and Ernalia Sri-Bintang, *Menggugat dakwaan subversi: Sri-Bintang Pamungkas di balik jeruji besi* (Jakarta: Yayasan Obor Indonesia, 2000), 71, 295, 358, 361; Biro Informasi dan Data, *Kliping tentang Timor Timur, Issue 498* (Jakarta: Centre for Strategic and International Studies, 2001), 113; Andi Mappetahang Fatwa, *Dari Cipinang ke Senayan: catatan gerakan reformasi dan aktivitas legislatif hingga ST MPR 2002* (Jakarta: Institute for Transformation Studies, 2003), 37, 346.

[104] Wilson recorded his words just shortly after the fall of the second Indonesian president: "I can tell you this: thirty minutes after Suharto stepped down [on May 21, 1998], the prison director [Sobari] came to us, all political prisoners, and said, 'Congratulations, Suharto has stepped down.' We also organized a party with the director! This means the bureaucrats in Cipinang prison support us also." https://wri-irg.org/en/story/1998/wilson-bin-nurtiyas-life-cipinang-prison. War Resisters' International, November 1, 1998. Gusmão, *A Woman of Independence*, 158, 204–7. The quote is taken from page 205.

indeed set free to enter a society that had been shaken by the resignation of Suharto on May 21, 1998 and a severe financial crisis.[105]

Reformasi and Referendum

The anger triggered by Indonesia's economic collapse in 1997–98 (13 percent GDP fall—the biggest of any open economy since World War II) created momentum of which the Indonesian solidarity movement gladly made use.[106] With more of their members released from prison and exiles like Yenny Damayanti returning from Europe, they started to lobby within the presidential palace. The comparison between human right abuses in East Timor and Java was central to their campaign. Yenny, for instance, joined the Women's Solidarity of Human Rights (SP, established in 1990) in June 1997 to underline how the surge of rape cases on Java—often aimed at citizens of Chinese descent—had its precedence in the systematic sexual abuse applied by the Indonesian army in Aceh and East Timor.[107]

The main advisor of the president—who, for political reasons, cannot be named in this paper—was invited to numerous informal meetings with several main figures of the Indonesian solidarity movement, who by now had all become acquainted with the stories of Xanana Gusmão.[108] Over coffee and cigarettes, they made Habibie's personal advisors and technocrats in his government aware of the plight of the East Timorese and convinced them that the special autonomy proposed on June 9, 1998 was not enough: a referendum was required to resolve an otherwise never-ending conflict. In addition to international pressure, this internal discussion encouraged the president to accept what had been unthinkable only a few years earlier when he allowed the referendum to occur in January 1999.[109]

---

[105] Hariyanto wrote the following on the series of releases of political prisoners: "Menjelang jejak pendapat bulan Agustus 1999, Xanana sudah bebas. Bahkan jauh sebelumnya dia bersama Joao sudah dipindah ke Rutan Khusus, di sebuah rumah di Jalan Percetakan Negara VII No 47. Ketika jejak pendapat dimenangkan rakyat Timor Leste, seluruh tahanan politik Timor Leste yang sempat ditempatkan berapa bulan di LP Cipinang juga ikut dibebaskan. Diantara mereka bahkan ada yang hukumannya mati." Hariyanto, *Kisah-Kisah di Balik Penjara* (December 10, 2019).

[106] Siegel, "Early Thoughts," 76–77.

[107] SP stands for Solidaritas Perempuan. "Kongres Solidaritas Perempuan: Perkosaan, Alat Teror Paling Keji," *Xpos* 27/I (June 4–9, 1998), 10–11.

[108] Gusmão was moved to a different prison in Jakarta on February 10, 1998 before being given safe haven in the British Embassy. Hariyanto, *Kisah-Kisah di Balik Penjara* (December 10, 2019); "Ensiklotimor: Cipinang," *Solid* 3 (1999), 45–46.

[109] Kai He, "Indonesia's Foreign Policy after Soeharto: International Pressure, Democratization, and Policy Change," *International Relations of the Asia-Pacific* 8, no. 1 (2008), 57–62. The lobby of the Indonesian activists led to an invitation to the East Timorese bishops Carlos Felipe Ximenes Belo (1948, Nobel Peace laureate October 1996) and Basílio do Nascimento (1950) in late December 1998. But Belo mistrusted Habibie and failed to show up. Interview with Yenny, June 25, 2020. As Dewi Fortuna Anwar, Habibie's Assistant Minister/State Secretary for Foreign Affairs, recalls: "It became clear that pro-independence East Timorese groups, as well as Portugal, viewed the special autonomy offer merely as an interim solution, the final solution being a referendum for self-determination at a later date." Dewi Fortuna Anwar, "The Habibie Presidency: Catapulting Towards Reform," in *Soeharto's New Order and Its Legacy Essays in Honour of Harold Crouch*, ed. Edward Aspinall and Greg Fealy (Canberra: Australian National University Press, 2010), 112; Bacharuddin Jusuf Habibie, *Detik-Detik yang Menentukan* (Jakarta: The Habibie Center, 2006), 136–39; Anwar, "The Habibie Presidency," 99, 104–5, 111–16.

Naturally, Habibie's reasons for calling a referendum were primarily to focus on the severe economic issues which had led to the downfall of his patron Suharto. Indonesian diplomats were fully occupied with answering questions on East Timor, whereas they wanted to address trade and investments to bolster their national economy which was in dire straits.[110] They were in need of a discourse which connected to the concerns on human right violations expressed by their foreign colleagues.

This discourse had been shaped over the course of five years by the Indonesian activists in underground media, international conferences, banners wielded during protest actions, and in interviews conducted behind bars. Their perspective on human rights was now offered on a plate to top officials of the Indonesian government, which had incarcerated activists for so long. It remained, however, at the heart a discourse on Indonesian concerns addressing the angry crowds that had roamed the streets of Jakarta throughout 1998 in search of a bowl of rice.[111] Human rights as understood by PIJAR, PRD, SPRIM, and SOLIDAMOR were part of the national reformation, as the activists sought to implement these "universal" principles into a new kind of nationalism for a reborn democratic nation that had risen or, at the very least, would rise—they hoped for a short moment in 1999—from the ashes of dictatorship and militarism.[112] The activists were quick to defend Habibie's decision and called on those who claimed the president was a "traitor" to reconsider the burden that East Timor had become and the senseless suffering thaty the conflict caused among East Timorese and Indonesian participants alike.[113]

In adapting their oppositional discourse to the needs of Indonesian diplomats for reviving the national economy, the Indonesian solidarity movement did increasingly incline to an uncritical, somewhat narrow, interpretation of what human rights entailed. The many different perspectives on the violence enacted on East Timor as well as other Indonesian provinces during the New Order regime were now reshaped into a single message that—as members of SOLIDAMOR claimed—resounded best in the "age of globalization of democratization." In reference to the National Socialist writing "Right or wrong, my country!" by the German author and former pastor Gustav Frenssen, they proclaimed a new era of "right is right, wrong is wrong, my country is my country."[114]

This crystallization of the polyphonic voices of resistance that had echoed from the ad hoc offices of samizdat weeklies, the conference speeches in Lisbon, and prisons

[110] Clinton Fernandes, "Indonesia's War against East Timor: How It Ended," *Small Wars & Insurgencies* 32, no. 6 (2021): 12–13.

[111] Aspinall, *Opposing Suharto*, 130–31.

[112] Bonar Naipospos formulated this idea as follows: "Yang harus dikembangkan adalah suatu konsepsi nasionalisme Indonesia baru yang memungkinkan pengaplikasian nilai-nilai demokrasi dan hak asasi manusia yang berlaku universal menjadi dasar dari kehidupan politik kita sehari-hari." Bonar Tigor Naipospos, "Nasionalisme Kita dan Timtim," *Solid* 6 (1999), 3.

[113] See footnote 114 and 116.

[114] SOLIDAMOR, "Hubungan Indonesia," 26. Note that Wilson had graduated with a thesis discussing national-socialism in the Netherlands Indies, see Wilson, "Curriculum Vitae"; Wilson, *Soekarno, komunis, dan fasis Orba* (Malang : Kelompok Intrans Publishing, 2015); Gustav Frenssen, *Recht oder Unrecht: Mein Land* (Berlin: G. Grote'sche Verlagshandlung, 1945); Anja Gatterbauer, *The Literary Work of Gustav Frenssen Motifs: Genre Definitions and Ideologies of a so Far Unknown Author* (Chisinau: LAP Lambert Academic Publishing, 2020).

cells of Cipinang inadvertently moved back to a conventional human rights discourse. The intercultural translation of what human rights entailed, which did occur within the many correspondences, publications, speeches, and blogs between 1994 and 1999 was now slowly reduced again to the original hegemonic concept of human rights as divided along state lines. Through Indonesia's international networks, they attempted to trade solidarity toward East Timor for solidarity towards Indonesia but did so along the lines of a conventional understanding of what human rights, globalization, and democratization were supposed to encompass. From this perspective, East Timor had been freed, but no apparent solution was offered to the ongoing exploitation of Javanese peasants, Acehnese and Papuan secessionist movements, and other suppressed Indonesian subjects other than the false hope of a democracy that all too soon turned into yet another neoliberal electoral ruling oligarchy, as soberly witnessed by Wilson, Tri Agus, and their activist peers in the years ahead.[115]

---

[115] Naturally, the "the non-material interests in the context of oligarchy" involve more people than merely the elite and does allow for their own types of resistance against nepotism and corruption, see Michele Ford and Thomas B. Pepinsky, "Preface," in *Beyond Oligarchy: Wealth, Power, and Contemporary Indonesian Politics,* ed. Michele Ford and Thomas B. Pepinsky (Ithaca, NY: Cornell University Press, 2014), ix; Michele Ford and Thomas B. Pepinsky, "Introduction: Beyond Oligarchy?," in Ford and Pepinsky, *Beyond Oligarchy,* 2–6; Jeffrey A. Winters, "Oligarchy and Democracy in Indonesia," *Indonesia* 96 (2013): 11–33; Boni Hargens, *Oligarchic Cartelization in Post-Suharto Indonesia* (Pittsburgh: Dorrance Publishing, 2021), 177; Wilson, "Poncke Princen," 1; Interview Tri Agus Susanto Siswowiharjo.

The Catholic Church's Campaign against the "Ethnic, Cultural and Religious Extinction of the Identity of the People" of East Timor: 1981–89

Michael Leach

Introduction

As the only public organization independent of the Indonesian regime, with well-established international links, the Catholic Church became a critical national institution in occupied East Timor in the 1980s and 1990s, offering a "sense of sanctuary" to the East Timorese in extraordinarily difficult circumstances (CAVR 2005, 3:99). As the Indonesian occupation of East Timor progressed, and the extent of human rights abuses became evident to the clergy, the Timorese church became an increasingly trenchant critic of the Indonesian regime and its destructive impact on East Timorese society. While the Vatican maintained a formal position of neutrality on the question of self-determination, the East Timorese church's tacit support for nationalism was evident by the early 1980s, and explicit by the end of the decade.

The Catholic Church hierarchy in East Timor launched a major campaign in the early 1980s that bore directly on issues of nationalism and national identity, arguing that Indonesian human rights abuses in the territory constituted a policy of the "ethnic, cultural and religious extinction of the identity of the people" (Catholic Commission

Michael Leach is Professor in Politics and International Relations, Swinburne University of Technology, Melbourne, author of Nation-Building and National Identity in Timor-Leste (Routledge)

for Justice, Development and Peace [CCJDP], [1985] 1993).[1] This campaign and the international networks it mobilized deeply stung the Indonesian administration and forced it to respond.

This paper first examines the Catholic Church's evolving role in the constitution of political community in East Timor through the Portuguese and Indonesian eras, arguing that it was seen as an essentially foreign institution until the Indonesian occupation. It then analyses the evolution of church campaigns over East Timorese "ethnic, cultural and religious identity" from 1981 onward and the way these campaigns strategically drew on newer developments in Catholic social doctrine, associated with Vatican II theology. These were employed to justify church support for nationalism, despite explicit prohibitions on political involvement. In particular, this paper focuses on a series of letters sent by successive Apostolic Administrators Martinho da Costa Lopes (1977–83) and Carlos Ximenes Belo (1983–2002), which expressed the evolution of this view among the East Timorese clergy. It is argued that these church campaigns over Timorese ethnic, cultural, and religious identity contributed substantially to the development of a national identity and reinforced claims of national self-determination. This campaign would prove central to the Catholic Church's evolution into an East Timorese national institution by the late 1980s.

The Colonial Church in Portuguese Timor

The Catholic Church in Portuguese Timor proved integral to the governing strategies of the colonial state, which evolved considerably over the long colonial era. In the era of indirect rule, at least from the time of Governor Affonso de Castro in the 1860s, the colonial church educated the sons of the local kings, the *liurai*, cultivating a small, educated elite strongly acculturated in the values of Portuguese society. In this way, Catholic conversions had a primarily political function, as the astute de Castro (1867, 29) observed.

> For a Timorese, to be Christian means to be a subject of His Majesty the King of Portugal, and this is the point politically. All things considered . . . religious conversions have more political than religious significance. Portugal acquired subjects but the Church did not increase its following since most of those converted were Christians in name only.

---

[1] This article avoids the term "cultural genocide," which had currency in 1980s solidarity campaigns, as it was not used by the Timorese Church itself, which instead referred to the "ethnic, cultural and religious extinction of the identity of the people" of East Timor. Ben Saul (2001, 45) analyzed the issue of genocide in East Timor, arguing that the conflict "most accurately qualifies as genocide against a 'political group,' or alternatively as 'cultural genocide,' yet neither of these concepts are explicitly recognised in international law." As such, prosecutions would likely be limited to "non-genocidal breaches of crimes against humanity, war crimes, and other gross violations of human rights." Nonetheless, Saul argued the term was normatively defensible, noting "it is persuasively arguable that 'cultural genocide' . . . was committed in East Timor, since Indonesia intentionally destroyed East Timorese group identity by forcibly assimilating the East Timorese into Indonesian institutions, politics, economy, culture and social life. Indonesia . . . destroyed traditional social patterns through forced relocations, breaking up family and village units, and resettling Indonesian migrants. In this sense, there is little real difference in outcome between acts of cultural genocide and acts of aggressive territorial and political control which similarly destroy a group's social characteristics" (41). The term "genocide" was also avoided by the Commission for Reception, Truth, and Reconciliation (CAVR) in Timor-Leste. Monsignor Martinho da Costa Lopes did however use the term, declaring, "I feel an urgent need to tell the whole world . . . about the genocide being practiced in Timor, so that, when we die, at least the whole world knows we died standing" (Lennox 2000, 174).

Later, as direct rule was imposed on the territory, the small group of church-educated *letrados* (literates) could be appointed to *chefe* positions to undermine the authority of rebellious *liurais*, or traditional kings (Araujo 1975, 4–5), providing new competition to traditional authorities within the colonial hierarchy.

Reversing the anti-clerical stance of the preceding Republican era, Salazar's *Estado Novo* lifted restrictions on religious orders that had prevailed from 1910 to 1926. From this point, the role of the religious missions as "agents of civilisation and of national influence" was explicitly acknowledged in Portugal's *Colonial Act* (Article 24, 1930). The corporatist *Estado Novo* signed a formal Concordat with the Vatican in 1940. Through the medium of the *Missionary Statute* of 1941, the Concordat gave the church exclusive control over the education of indigenous people within the Portuguese colonies, in return for supporting Portuguese colonial ideologies. The church was viewed as a prime agent of civilization, and its colleges became key sites for acculturating Timorese elites to Portuguese culture. As Alexandre Fernandes explains, the Concordat specifically envisaged the role of the church as one reinforcing Portuguese colonial rule, making Christian and Portuguese subjects of Timorese converts, as "two features of the same project" (2014, 21, author's trans.). To these ends, the concordat required Catholic missions in Portuguese colonies to be administered primarily by Portuguese missionaries (Art. 2); and for diocese boundaries to respect the boundaries of Portuguese colonies (Art. 6). Bishops appointed by the Holy See to the colonies had to be approved by the Portuguese government (Art. 7) and the church was obliged to give Portuguese classes in schools (Art. 16). For its part, the Portuguese state was obliged to subsidize the missions, donate land for the construction of mission buildings, and pay pensions (Art. 13) to retired clergy. These links between church and colonial state were openly celebrated in the earliest editions of the Timorese church's journal *Seara*, with articles such as "To Evangelize Is to Nationalize," acknowledging that the church sought to make good Portuguese citizens as well as Christian subjects (*Seara*, September 9, 1949; quoted in Fernandes 2014, author's trans.):

> The missionary conscience is not just a duty; It is also a national duty. . . . But Portugal, in its missions, not only evangelizes, it civilizes as well (when the church evangelizes, it always civilizes)! Missionaries are not, of course, the only civilizers, but they are the best.

The Late Colonial Church: Vatican II and the "Right to Culture"

By the 1960s, however, the influence of the Second Vatican Council saw the Catholic Church increasingly seeking to distance itself from colonial states. As Fernandes notes (2014, 126), though the conservative church in Dili was hardly the most enthusiastic proponent of this global trend, articles in *Seara* concerning new Portuguese legislation, and other concerns of the colonial state, became notably rarer. Other signs of change were evident in the Timorese church's attempts to "culturalize" its pastoral activities, with prayers and marriage rites translated into Tetum and other local languages and bilingual Portuguese/Tetum articles appearing for the first time in the late 1960s (2014, 131). A 1969 article, "The Church and Cultures," signaled the profound implications of the shift in Rome for relations with the Portuguese colonial state. Discussing the "reasons for missionary adaptation," it argued (Fernandes 2014, 130, author's trans.):

One of the main natural rights of society is the right to their own culture, to their national genius, to their character. Pius XII clearly says: the right to life, the right to respect and good name, the right to a character and a culture of their own. . . . Missionary work is a paradox; on the one hand, natural law imposes on missionary duty to respect the right of a people in their own culture and their national character; on the other hand the mission was mandated to transform the world.

As the Australian Bishop Hilton Deakin (2017, 122–23) notes, in the wake of the Vatican II era (1962–65), the Catholic Church moved from a "Eurocentric and elitist" view of missionary work, which saw traditional cultures as "pagan," to one that recognized the rights of peoples to their own culture, within a broader shift to the recognition of human rights (125). Following these trends, by 1975 the church in Timor—and the more liberal Jesuit order in particular—had become a "cautious agent for social and political change" in Portuguese Timor (Carey 1999, 79). Held in higher regard than the secular authorities, priests were often able to intercede on behalf of parishioners in disputes with the Portuguese administration or with the *liurai*, and the church made efforts to mitigate the worst of Portuguese forced labor schemes. The degree of trust this built with ordinary Timorese was evident in conversions in the late colonial era, rising from an estimated 13 percent of the population in 1952 to 30 percent by 1973. Nonetheless, the conduct of mass in Portuguese and Latin meant the church was still regarded as a "foreign institution" by a majority of East Timorese (Carey 1999, 79), and conversions were often shallow, with double marriage ceremonies and *adat* beliefs the norm for rural converts. As Deakin noted, while the church was increasingly expected to help with injustice or corruption from the *liurai* or Portuguese officials, it still "operated from *within* the ruling system" (2017, 111). This would change fundamentally in the Indonesian era, as the church began to intercede on behalf of Timorese parishioners from outside the system of government.

The Catholic Church in the 1980s: An Emerging National Institution

The Indonesian invasion of 1975 and forced integration of the territory saw the church transform its relationship with the state once again, in ways that would have profound consequences for nation-building and national identity in East Timor. Once again, an occupying power sought to recruit religious institutions to consolidate its rule and to help develop a sense of political community that supported the regime. Indonesian attempts to integrate the Timorese diocese into the Indonesian Catholic Church—and their ultimate failure—would prove critical to the East Timorese struggle for self-determination, as the Timorese church evolved to become a trenchant opponent of the occupying power. The church soon proved to be the only institution capable of affording a degree of protection to East Timorese and by the 1980s would be seen as a unifying forum for expressing the common suffering of East Timor's ethnolingusitic groups (Anderson 1993). The adoption of a Catholic identity carried strategic nationalist dimensions, differentiating the East Timorese from the majority religion of their occupier and from predominately Protestant west Timor. For ordinary East Timorese, conversion became a popular mode of reinforcing a separate sense of identity, available to all, and sanctioned by the logic of the Indonesian state, which required citizens to affiliate to one of the five official religions in its formal identification card system (Anderson 1993). These developments would greatly increase the church's popularity and domesticate it into a truly national institution. By as early as 1980 the numbers of Catholics had increased dramatically to 50 percent, up from an estimated 30 percent before 1975 (Walsh 1980).

In 1981, after the use of Portuguese was banned by the Indonesian authorities, the Apostolic Administrator Martinho da Costa Lopes successfully petitioned the Vatican to adopt Tetun as the language of the East Timorese church. The clergy's rejection of liturgical Indonesian proved a hugely significant milestone, vital to the "cultural survival of the Timorese people" (CAVR 2005, 3:99). In place by 1983, this policy had "profoundly nationalizing effects" (Anderson 1993, 7), transforming Tetun's status from a territorial lingua franca to a national language and extending its reach beyond traditional district boundaries. Estimates hold that just 50 percent of East Timorese were fluent in Tetun in 1975 (Ramos-Horta 1987: 205), rising to well over 80 percent by the end of the Indonesian era. The adoption of Tetun also firmly domesticated the Catholic Church as an East Timorese institution, making it the prime institutional forum for expressing a national identity; just as schooling, media, and other public institutions attempted to "Indonesianize" the population. As the church openly defied "Bahasaization" (Lutz 1995, 4), it also continued to use Portuguese in its external communications, in the same manner as the resistance. Examples of congregations refusing to join in singing hymns in Indonesian with visiting Indonesian seminarians highlight the active politics of liturgical languages in this era (Carey 1999, 85–86).

Also critical to developing and maintaining a sense of a distinct political community was the refusal of the local Diocesan church to integrate itself with the Indonesian Catholic Church.[2] As the Vatican did not recognize the forced integration of East Timor, it remained a separate ecclesiastical province throughout the occupation, dealing directly with Rome. The lack of accountability to the Indonesian church would prove a constant hindrance to the Indonesian authorities in their attempts to convert the clergy to the cause of integration.

Meanwhile, conversions to Catholicism continued apace. In 1983, The *Timor Information Service* (1983, 7) reported that "several thousand people a month are being converted to Catholicism, which would appear to be their way of rejecting integration with Indonesia." Notably, adult baptisms and conversions occurred despite the considerable efforts of Protestant churches to evangelize in East Timor, with the tacit support of Indonesian authorities, which continued to mistrust the spread of Catholicism in East Timor (see also Feijo 2011). This attitude was evident in the banning of Bible discussion groups, based on fears that politics would instead be discussed (Carey 1999, 87), and in close surveillance of the church leadership.

Despite the Indonesian state's efforts to socialize a new generation of East Timorese youth, the church's role in education would also prove a significant obstacle. As Gunn suggests (2006, 71), the Catholic Church's network—tolerated owing to perennial teacher shortages—was an important "parallel" institution in occupied East Timor that facilitated a cautious level of diversity in educational experiences. Key examples include the Externato Sao Jose, the sole Portuguese language school, which church authorities

---

[2] Unlike the Diocesan Church, the Jesuit order in Dili did operate under the jurisdiction of Indonesian Province.

succeeded in reopening for students awaiting expatriation to Portugal. The school operated until shortly after the Santa Cruz massacre of 1991, with notable graduates including the main organizer of the Santa Cruz protests, Gregorio Saldanha.

In sum, by the late 1980s the combined effect of these developments was to make the East Timorese, in Anthony D. Smith's terms, a religious *ethnie*, or ethnic core. Where in the late 1970s East Timorese nationalism was at best an anticolonial ideology uniting some educated segments of East Timor's various ethnolinguistic groups, new ethnic forms of commonality would be evident by the 1980s in a predominantly Catholic, Tetun-speaking society (Leach 2017, 12). As Smith (1987, 124) argues, it is religious *ethnies* that tend to survive best in the absence of an independent state, especially where a distinct liturgical language and organized priesthood provide a durable institutional basis to a separate sense of identity.

These developments in the Timorese church occurred at the same time as the East Timorese resistance was fundamentally reorganized under Xanana Gusmão's leadership throughout the 1980s. This decade saw a broad shift in strategy toward *apartidismo* (non-partisanship), with the military wing of the resistance, FALINTIL, separating formally from the original party of independence, FRETILIN, and the formation of a broad front for all nationalists, the National Council of the Maubere Resistance (Conselho Nacional da Resistencia Maubere [CNRM]) in 1988. These developments slowly moved the secular resistance away from 1970s polarities and facilitated a more productive de facto relationship with the church. With tacit support for nationalism, the church launched a major campaign in the early 1980s accusing Indonesia of instituting policies leading to the "ethnic, cultural and religious extinction of the identity of the people" of East Timor.

The Church Campaign: 1981–85

The East Timorese clergy issued several statements on the situation in East Timor throughout the first half of the decade, starting with a letter to the Conference of Indonesian Major Religious Superiors in 1981,[3] followed by a 1983 statement disseminated to Catholic Bishop Conferences throughout the world. Of particular significance was the 1985 Statement to the Council of Priests on the "ethnic, cultural and religious extinction of the identity of the people of East Timor" (CCJDP 1993). Though it would openly support self-determination by the end of the decade, the church at this time strategically emphasized issues of cultural identity and human rights over more overtly political themes.

Following the retirement of Bishop Ribeiro in 1977, whose tenure represented the legacy of the concordat in colonial Timor,[4] the first statement was cosigned by the first indigenous head of the Timorese diocese, Monsignor Martinho da Costa Lopes, in July 1981. In a criticism of the Indonesian church and Vatican's silence over the human rights abuses, Lopes spoke of the destructive impact of Indonesia's security policies and mass population transfers (CCJDP [1981] 1993, 14):

---

[3] This document was prepared by the "Religious of East Timor" for presentation at the Conference of Indonesian Major Religious Superiors in 1981.

[4] In January 1975 Ribeiro had warned of "materialistic and atheistic communism and socialistic Marxism which is seeking to extinguish the positive values of the Timorese people." See Jardine 1992.

> . . . the people's way of life has been turned upside down and the basis of community life has been destroyed. Masses of the population have been forced to shift in large numbers to places far away and unknown . . . apart from having lost all their possessions, there is alienation and disintegration of families.

The letter then went on to document the forced participation of male Timorese in Indonesian security operations, including the notorious "fence of legs" campaign, and condemned the way the military was monopolizing all the resources of the territory, subtly referencing Indonesian military responsibility for famine that plagued East Timor in the late 1970s.

Significantly, Lopes and his later replacement, Carlos Ximenes Belo, reported directly to the Vatican, via the Nuncio in Jakarta (CAVR 2013, 678), rather than through the Indonesian church. This was an important structural factor that indicated the Vatican's formal view that the political status of the territory was unsettled, awaiting an act of self-determination. With the much larger Indonesian church in mind, however, the Vatican did not make this position public (CAVR 2013, 678), and many senior Vatican officials in practice considered the occupation a fait accompli. Reflecting on these factors, the 1981 letter from the Timorese clergy made it plain that the church in Timor was being pressured to join with the Indonesian Catholic Church to further the goals of integration:

> we are aware that we are being "persuaded" to set up links with the Indonesian Church, because it is the Church that is closest to us, and the one the government and army have authorised to maintain a closer relationship with us.

The letter went on to express the clergy's sadness that their relations with the wider "universal Church" had been "suddenly curtailed," noting that they had, along with the people of East Timor, "been thrown into a vacuum and alienated for 6 years, so we have become the silent Church of East Timor" (ETAN 1994, 157). The clergy expressed particular disappointment that the "Indonesian Church and the universal Roman Church" had not openly stated their solidarity with the church and people of East Timor: "Perhaps this has been the heaviest blow for us . . . we feel stunned by this silence which seemed to allows us to die deserted." As Kohen notes (1999, 116) the Timorese clergy were clearly arguing the Vatican could have mobilized international public opinion but had hitherto failed to act. Lopes's outspoken stance caused consternation in Jakarta and undermined the Vatican's preference for quiet diplomacy (CAVR 2005, 3:99). Indeed, Lopes's resignation in 1983 suggested the Vatican had bowed to pressure (Carey 1999, 83), though his replacement from 1983 to 2002, Carlos Ximenes Belo, would become equally critical of the occupation, despite increasing intimidation and violence directed toward the clergy.

For example, letters from the new Apostolic administrator Belo wrote reached the French and Dutch Catholic Churches in 1984, urging that any resolution to the conflict in East Timor must be "political and diplomatic . . . with respect for the right to self-determination" (Taylor 1990, 49). A more significant statement would follow in 1985, as the Timorese Council of Priests issued a seven-page statement of principle. "Having experienced with the people all the events which since 1975" they wrote, "the Church bears anxious witness to facts that are slowly leading to the ethnic, cultural and religious extinction of the identity of the people of East Timor" (East Timor Report 1985, 2). Cosigned by Belo, it argued forcefully that the fabric of East Timorese society was "gravely threatened and violated" by regular military offensives, executions, arbitrary arrests, forced conscription, the concentration of the population in resettlement camps, and the exclusion of East Timorese from key positions in the administration.

The clergy cited Pope John Paul II's 1984 comments to the Indonesian Ambassador to the Vatican, requesting that "particular consideration . . . be given in every circumstance to the ethnic, political and cultural identity of the people" (Taylor 1999, 154). Though the Vatican subsequently dropped the word "political," there is little doubt that the church campaign was instrumental in the Indonesian offer of special autonomy in 1986, discussed further below. The 1985 statement, which Belo was later forced to repudiate, also directly addressed of the issue of the religious identity of the population, objecting to the fact that Christianity had been put on an equal footing to other religions, despite the presence of 400,000 Catholics (*East Timor Report* 1985, 1).[5] The latter position openly challenged fundaments of Indonesian state ideology and represented an outright denunciation of the practice of transmigration. Though focused on culture and religion, there was no escaping the church's implicit position that East Timor represented a distinct political community, with differences that Indonesia's unitary, multi-religious state could not integrate.

In perhaps its most powerful rhetoric, the council's letter argued that a distinct East Timorese cultural identity was being "progressively destroyed" (*East Timor Report* 1985, 2):

> There is a Timorese culture made up of words, attitudes, emotions, reactions . . . ways of being and seeing the world. It is in these things that the people recognize their own culture and their own identity. The attempt to Indonesianise the Timorese people through powerful *Pancasila* . . . campaigns, schooling and media, by divorcing the people from their own *weltanschauung* (world view) represents a slow assassination of Timorese culture. To kill their culture is to kill the people themselves.

The challenge to Indonesia's integration of its restive province could scarcely have been more overt. The Council of Priests then went to some lengths to note that a distinctive East Timorese culture had developed over centuries, comprising indigenous traditions and customs "in contact with Portuguese civilization and under the influence of Christianity." This particular formulation of East Timorese identity explicitly countered Indonesian notions of "reuniting" populations separated by the colonial era and reflected similar positions on East Timorese identity advanced by the independence movement generally (see Leach 2017, 87–88). "Conscious of its mission," they wrote, "the church wishes to set down what it feels to be vital and urgent for the defence and safeguarding of the fundamental values and human rights of the people of East Timor as well as their identity at this historical moment in time." As Deakin noted, the clergy's 1985 letter drew explicitly on developments in Catholic social teaching that had taken the church from Concordat-era understandings of "civilizing missions" to one that recognized the rights of people to their own a right to "national culture" and character.

---

[5] "To ignore the religious traditions of the Timorese, even that of animism, and to attribute the same standing to Christianity as to other religions, is an attempt to destroy the people's beliefs." (*East Timor Report* 1985, 1)

Links with Catholic Social Doctrine

In April 1985 Belo drafted a letter to young Timorese. In it he noted the importance of national personality, reflecting on church encyclicals to argue that the narrow benefits of development offered by the Indonesians were no substitute for the right of wider political participation in society. Citing *Populorum Progressio* (1967), he argued that development could not be reduced to simple economic growth and must "foster the development of each person and of the whole person" (Timor Link 1985, 14). Drawing on the Second Vatican Council document *Guadium et Spes* (1965), Belo then argued that it was both a right and duty "to contribute to the true progress of their own community" and that this right should be recognized by secular authority (Timor Link 1985, 4), Belo went on to draw on church teachings to argue that Timor was a nation, and young people owe a duty to it:

> As individuals we form part of a community. We are born in a particular territory called Timor. For this Timor we must nurture love, devotion and zeal. The love of one's native land, a sense of its history, the defence of all that makes up the culture, progress, greatness and survival of Timor, all this is patriotism. Patriotism is a universal human attribute, and the most characteristic and the noblest virtue of a civilised person. The church calls on all, particularly Christians, to love their country: they "must cultivate a generous and loyal spirit of patriotism . . . and give an example by their sense of responsibility and their service of the common good." (*Gaudiam et Spes* 75)

In more strident tones, Belo argued that the church should not fail to recognize that the East Timorese people also possess these universal and inalienable attributes of peoples, including rights to self-determination and independence, "since many of the Catholic Christians who have already died for the liberation of their country and not to be subjected to a new colonial regime" (Timor Link 1985, 4). This letter was notable for repeatedly adopting the nationalist term "the Maubere people."

Internal Church Correspondence

In a lesser-known letter dated February 17, 1985, Belo reported to Monsenhor Pablo Puente, the Apostolic Nuncio of the Holy See to Jakarta. Intended for the narrower audience of the Vatican representatives, this report included a frank characterization of the historical role of the church in Timor, divided into three distinct periods. Belo noted that "proper quality Evangelism" commenced only in 1875, producing some 30,000 Catholics at the eve of World War II; but that major improvements in the church's approach had seen 220,000 converts, or 30 percent of the population by 1975 (1985, 2).

Belo's comments on the period from 1974 to 1976 were brief and covered the invasion, and the consequent end of the Concordat, resulting in the departure of many missionaries and closure of schools. He then canvassed the new direct relationship between the Diocese of Dili and the Holy See and the appointment of the first indigenous Apostolic Administrator, his predecessor Martinho da Costa Lopes. Most interestingly, Belo describes the church in 1985 as "flourishing," having changed the "religious panorama" of the territory to one that now has "more Catholics than animists," with an estimated 75 percent of the population now converted. Belo (1985, 3) frankly noted that many newer converts "experience the dangers from [sic] superficial Christianity" and lack "real cultural points of view and deep association" with the church. These comments suggested that church arguments concerning the religious identity in the territory were—at least in part—strategic in nature and mobilized to nationalist ends.

Belo then noted two "delicate problems" concerning the religious composition of the territory. The first was the growing number of Muslims that had settled following integration, which he estimated at 15,000, including some local converts. The second was the rise in the number of Protestants, with "ample devotees." Belo also frankly discussed the syncretic nature of Timorese Catholicism, worshipping both "God and 'Maromak' (the one supreme being in animist religions) at the same time in the practice of religion." In this respect—and in an argument that perhaps most forcefully supported notions of a distinctive religious identity in East Timor—Belo noted that the church "has a true personality" in East Timor that was "enrooted [sic] in the people" (1985, 3).

Belo went on to alert the Nuncio to two other problems facing the Diocese: the presence of the Indonesian Catholic clergy and the operation of the Indonesian doctrine of *Pancasila*. On the first issue, Belo suggested the presence of "dualism" in the Catholic clergy would cause apprehension between Christians and asked the Nuncio "what is the solution?" (1985, 4). Belo also noted the absence of a permanent Bishop, suggesting an Ecclesiastical Province of Timor with the Diocese head in Dili, which could have two more seats in Baucau and Maliana (as it does today). Significantly, Belo argued that all the Timorese missions form a "unitary body in their type of faith and pastoral procedures" and furthermore that "the missionary influence is Portuguese" and one that "does not correspond much with the characteristics of the adjoining Diocese of Nusatenggara Timor"; adding that this was moreover an opinion held by the clergy at large (1985, 4).

Finally, the letter reflected in-depth on the issue of respect for the cultural identity of the Timorese. Here, in confidential correspondence, Belo divided the population between the "civilized class" and the population in general, noting that only the educated and literate were in daily contact with the Indonesians. For Belo, this group did not live by the "proper Timorese culture" and dwelled daily in Indonesian-dominated institutions. As such, their prime contact with Timorese culture was through the church itself, with its Tetun liturgy. Belo also commented on the way this group perceived traditional customs and dances, under the gaze of the Indonesians:

> The standard of the folklore, of the practices and customs, and the traditions that are indigenous . . . because it is of a defeated people it is not developed, not enriched, it is not preserved. They follow the things of Java and Bali. . . . In our schools the students feel inferior when they present an indigenous dance . . . all laugh.

Belo contrasted this group with the "illiterate majority" of East Timorese, who "were never connected with the Portuguese culture, [and] are also not connected with the Indonesians, because of the Indonesian treatment." In another acknowledgment of the thin nature of many Catholic conversions, Belo noted that this group continues with its own animist customs and that it is "this category of people the Church is trying to improve, christianise and conserve" (1985, 5).

The 1989 Visit of John Paul II

Carlos Ximenes Belo was formally declared a bishop in 1988 and on February 6, 1989, defiantly called on UN Secretary General Perez de Cuellar to conduct a guided process of decolonization of East Timor, requesting a United Nations referendum on self-determination. "The decolonisation process of Portuguese Timor," he wrote, "has still not been resolved by the UN, and it should not be allowed to be forgotten ... I ask that the Secretary General initiate in Timor that which is the most usual and democratic decolonisation process, the holding of a REFERENDUM . . . in the meantime we are dying as a people and as a nation" (ETAN [1989] 1994, 158). This letter, and others like it written to the Pope and the Portuguese President (CAVR 2013, 681), angered the Indonesian authorities, and the bishop was subjected to anonymous death threats. The Pope's visit in October of 1989 would prove a signal moment in Timorese aspirations for self-determination. As one who attended the Papal mass recalled in CAVR hearings (2013, 683), "we felt very proud. If he'd only come to Indonesia, it would have meant he accepted East Timor as part of Indonesia, but he singled us out. It gave us a lot of hope." The Pope was subsequently interviewed on Portuguese radio, making comments that reflected the position of Catholic social doctrine on national culture (CAVR 2013, 683):

> I wish for that community . . . that it should be able to live in accord with its own principles and customs, its language and its own culture, its own traditions and religion. The political problems is a problem to be taken up in another place: The United Nations. And I hope . . . that the problem of Timor-Leste will be resolved in accord with the principles of justice and human and national rights.

By the time of Pope John Paul II's visit, who remained the only world leader to visit East Timor during the occupation (CAVR 2013, 675), the Indonesian administration would consider the Catholic Church in Timor the primary obstacle to integration (Taylor 1999, 157). Xanana Gusmão would later describe the church as the "backbone of the resistance" (Carey 1999, 82). It is important to note that while the East Timorese resistance lauded the role of Pope John Paul II, it continued to be critical of the Vatican bureaucracy, which never mobilized its resources fully to support self-determination, and, given its sensitivity to the church in Indonesia, gave limited public coverage of the issue (CAVR 2013, 683–85). The CAVR report concluded that while the Vatican did not desert the church in East Timor, its repeated attempts to silence those speaking out meant its support for the East Timorese clergy's campaigns was ultimately limited.

Indonesian Contestation of Church Campaigns

Throughout this period, the Indonesian government attempted to counter the claims being advanced by the Timorese church. These attempts took three key forms. First, Indonesian government publications through the 1980s and 1990s attempted to rebut the charge of "ethnic, cultural and religious extinction" being leveled by the Catholic Church. This usually took the form of emphasizing cultural similarities between East Timor and neighboring societies; or denying that East Timorese cultural differences were exceptional among Indonesia's diverse ethnic groups. In 1992 the government publication "East Timor: Building for the Future" declared (1992, vi):

The allegation that the East Timorese are different from other Indonesians ignores the fact that Indonesia is a land of diversity comprising 300 distinct ethnic groups . . . people of the same Melanesian ancestry, and with the same culture, language and customs, inhabit the western part of Timor and the surrounding islands of Indonesia.

Other publications sought to deny the impact of 450 years of Portuguese influence and contact, with the Teachers Association of Indonesia (1993, 19) arguing that "promoting the culture of Timor is nothing new for Indonesia, because East Timor shares the same small island and culture as West Timor. Only these detractors pretended to perceive that the two are different."

Second, the Indonesian government proposed a form of "special autonomy" in East Timor in 1986 (Taylor 1990, 60–61), arising from at UN-sponsored talks with Portugal. Under the short-lived proposal, Portuguese and Tetun could be "spoken freely," and street names would be returned to original Portuguese. Aside from these minor cultural concessions, Indonesia promised to install more East Timorese in positions of authority in the provincial administration and a full transfer of security to the territorial 744 and 745 battalions of East Timorese recruits. In a clear attempt to disrupt the growing alliance between the East Timorese resistance and the Catholic Church, the Indonesian offer also promised special status to the church in the territory: effectively offering to recognize a Catholic religious identity (Gusmão [1987] 2000, 87).[6] There were also contemporary suggestions that transmigration policies might be reviewed,[7] to undermine church claims of a "cultural extinction" in occupied East Timor. These offers clearly constituted Jakarta's political response to the church campaigns of the early 1980s. The leader of the resistance, Xanana Gusmão, dismissed these offers as "illusory," attacking the assumption that the right to speak Portuguese and Tetun could preserve the historical and cultural identities of the East Timorese, or that halting transmigration would preserve its ethnic identity while the nation remained forcibly integrated. In a letter to the Australian Senator Gordon McIntosh, Gusmão described these as "historical palliatives" that could not meet the Timorese people's "sacred aspirations" to independence, nor reflect their "true . . . socio-cultural identity" (Gusmão 1988, 3–4).

Finally, Indonesian attempts to integrate the Timorese diocese into the Indonesian Episcopal Conference continued throughout the occupation and were openly acknowledged as a strategy to facilitate political integration. Kohen (1999, 131) records that the Indonesian Conference of Catholic bishops had expressed the view upon Belo's ascension in 1983 that it was "only a matter of time" until the Diocese in Dili joined the Indonesian church. In 1994, the Chairman of the Golkar party visited Dili and promised a new cathedral if the diocese agreed to integrate with the Indonesian Bishops' Conference (ETAN 1994, 11). A similar promise that new Salesian missionaries would be allowed to enter was made on the same condition. As ETAN reported at the time,

---

[6] There is some evidence that this offer was treated seriously by Bishop Belo, at least initially. According to Niner (2009, 109), at a secret meeting with Gusmão in 1986, the Bishop had spoken favorably of the autonomy proposal, putting the two at odds; Belo's growing profile as a defender of human rights notwithstanding.

[7] In 1984, East Timor was declared open to sponsored transmigrants from elsewhere in Indonesia, with "guided villages" established for those resettled by the government (Jannisa 1997, 159). At its peak, the numbers of sponsored transmigrasi were estimated in the tens of thousands, especially in the districts of Cova Lima, Maliana, and Manatuto.

Indonesian journalists covering the visit noted openly that religious integration would represent "the last stage in the overall integration process of East Timor" (ETAN 1994, 11). These perceived links between religious and political integration were made quite plain, with the Secretary of the Episcopal Conference, Monsignor Situmorang, stating, "We have always wanted East Timor to participate in our Episcopal Conference, not only for nationalist reasons, but also because of the ecclesiastic ties between us." Such ties, he noted, would "intensify the Timorese's feeling of belonging to Indonesia." For its part, the Vatican continued to reject these overtures, arguing that no change should occur until the status of East Timor had been settled internationally (ETAN 1994, 11).

Conclusion

This paper has examined the significance of the East Timorese church's campaigns over the "ethnic, cultural and religious extinction of the identity of the people" from 1981 onward and the way they strategically drew on development Catholic social doctrine to buttress the claims of the East Timorese people to their right to self-determination. Drawing on the longer history of the church's attempts to support the identity projects of the colonial state, it has also examined a major transformation in local perceptions of the church from that of a foreign institution in the late colonial era, to a forum for expressing core elements of an emergent East Timorese national identity in the 1980s and 1990s. In this process, and despite inconsistent support from the Vatican, the Timorese church became a defender of the East Timorese people's right to their own culture and national character and ultimately, a persistent and effective international advocate for self-determination.

Postscript

In late September 2022, reports emerged that historical accusations of sexual abuse of boys had been leveled by several Timorese complainants against the former Bishop Carlos Ximenes Belo (Lingsma 2022). The Vatican subsequently confirmed it had received evidence of the accusations in 2019 and had sanctioned Belo the following year, including limitations to the exercise of his ministry and the prohibition of voluntary contact with minors.

References

Anderson, B. 1993. "Imagining East Timor" *Arena Magazine* 4 (April–May): 23–27.

Araujo, A. 1975. *Timorese Elites*. Translated by J. M. Alberto. Edited by J. Jolliffe and B. Reece. Canberra: J. Jolliffe and B. Reece.

Belo, Carlos X. 1985. Letter to Monsenhor Pablo Puente, Nuncio Apostolic, Jakarta. February 17.

Carey, P. 1999. "The Catholic Church, Religious Revival, and the Nationalism Movement in East Timor, 1985–85." *Indonesia and the Malay World* 28 (8): 77–95.

Castro, A. de. 1867. *As possessões Portuguezas na Oceania*. Lisbon: Imprensa Nacional.

Catholic Commission for Justice, Development and Peace. 1993. *The Church and East Timor: A Collection of Documents by National and International Church Agencies*. Melbourne: Catholic Commission for Justice, Development and Peace.

CAVR. 2005. *Chega!: The Report of the Commission for Reception, Truth, and Reconciliation in Timor-Leste*. Dili: CAVR.

———. 2013. *Chega!: The Report of the Commission for Reception, Truth and Reconciliation in Timor-Leste*. Dili: CAVR. English translation.

Deakin, Hilton. 2017. *Bonded through Tragedy, United in Hope*. Mulgrave, AUS: Garrett Publishing.

ETAN. 1994. "The Church in East Timor—Voice of a Silenced People." *Documents on East Timor from PeaceNet and Connected Computer Networks*. Volume 31, June 30–September 15, 1994, 158. https://www.etan.org/etanpdf/timordocs/timmas31%2094-09-15.pdf.

Feijo, R. 2011. "Tradução e falsos amigos: Considerações em torno dos 'nomes portugueses' em Timor-Leste." In *Ita maun alin: o livro do irmão mais novo. afinidades antropológicas em torno de Timor-Leste*, edited by Kelly C. Silva and Lucío Sousa Lisbon: Colibri, pp. 87-111.

Fernandes, Alexandre. 2014. "Em searas do Timor Português: Um estudo sobre as práticas de mediação da Diocese de Díli no período colonial (1949–1973)." Master's thesis, University of Brasilia.

Gunn, G. C. 2006. *Timor-Leste: An Anthropology of War and Liberation*. Southeast Asian Studies Series 38. Nagasaki: Nagasaki University Press.

Gusmão, X. 1988. Letter to Senator Gordon McIntosh. https://timorarchives.files.wordpress.com/2016/05/xanana-mcintosh-letter-1988-eng1.pdf.

———. 2000. *To Resist Is to Win: The Autobiography of Xanana Gusmão with Selected Letters and Speeches*. Edited by S. Niner. Melbourne: Aurora/David Lovell Publishing.

Jannisa, G. 1997. *The Crocodile's Tears: East Timor in the Making*. Lund: Lund University Press.

Jardine, Matthew. 1992. "The Catholic Church in East Timor." *Documents on East Timor from PeaceNet*. Volume 18, October 5–November 30, 21. https://www.etan.org/etanpdf/timordocs/timmas18%2092-11-30.pdf.

Kohen, Arnold. 1999. *From the Place of the Dead: The Epic Struggles of Bishop Belo of East Timor*. New York: St Martin's Press.

Leach, M. 2017. *Nation-Building and National Identity in Timor-Leste*. London: Routledge.

Lennox, Rowena. 2000. *Fighting Spirit of East Timor: The Life of Martinho da Costa Lopes*. London: Pluto Press.

Lingsma, Tjitska. 2022. "Investigation–Sexual Abuse of Children by Nobel Peace Prize Winner Bishop Belo: 'What I Want Is Apologies.'" *De Groene Amsterdammer*, September 28.

Lutz, N. 1995. "Colonization, Decolonization and Integration: Language Policies in East Timor, Indonesia." Paper presented at the American Anthropological Association conference, Chicago, November 20. http://www.ci.uc.pt/timor/language.htm.

Niner, S. 2009. *Xanana: Leader of the Struggle for Independent Timor-Leste*. North Melbourne: Australian Scholarly Publishing.

Ramos-Horta, J. 1987. *Funu: The Unfinished Saga of East Timor*. Trenton: The Red Sea Press.

Republic of Indonesia. 1992. *East Timor: Building for the Future. Issues and Perspectives*. Jakarta: Department of Foreign Affairs, Republic of Indonesia.

Saul, Ben. 2001. "Was the Conflict in East Timor 'Genocide' and Why Does It Matter?" *Melbourne Journal of International Law* 2 (2): 1–46.

Smith, A. 1987. *The Ethnic Origins of Nations*. Oxford: Blackwell.

Taylor, J. G. 1990. *The Indonesian Occupation of East Timor 1974–1989: A Chronology*. London: Catholic Institute for International Relations.

———. 1999. *East Timor: The Price of Freedom*. London: Zed Books.

Teachers Association of the Republic of Indonesia. 1993. *East Timor: The Rising Province of Indonesia*. Jakarta: PGRI.

Timor Information Service. 1983. "East Timorese Resistance Continues." https://chartperiodicals
        .files.wordpress.com/2010/09/tis_40_p.pdf.
Timor Link. 1985. "Mgr Belo's Letter to Young Timorese." no. 4, December, 1–8. https://vuir.vu
        .edu.au/25943/1/TIMORLINK4_compressed.pdf.
Walsh. P. 1980. *Notes on the East Timor Issue Based on International Visit 3.6.80–18.8.80.* Fitzroy:
        Action for World Development.